W.H. Strobridge

Catalogue of oriental wares and antiques

W.H. Strobridge

Catalogue of oriental wares and antiques

ISBN/EAN: 9783741139666

Manufactured in Europe, USA, Canada, Australia, Japa

Cover: Foto ©ninafisch / pixelio.de

Manufactured and distributed by brebook publishing software
(www.brebook.com)

W.H. Strobridge

Catalogue of oriental wares and antiques

CATALOGUE

OF

Oriental Wares and Antiquities.

CONSISTING OF

LACQUERS; CARVINGS; EMBROIDERIES; CLOISONNE-
ENAMELS; PORCELAIN; EARTHEN-WARE; ORNAMENT-
AL AND SACRED VASES, CANDLESTICKS, CENSERS, AND
OTHER IMPLEMENTS IN BRONZE; ETC., ETC.

Old China, Delft, Faience, and other Rare Pottery,

FROM

GERMAN, FRENCH, ITALIAN, SPANISH, ENGLISH, AND OTHER
FACTORIES, MANY OF THEM NO LONGER IN EXISTENCE.

Textile and other Fabrics,

FROM TURKEY, PERSIA, AND ALGERIA,

SUCH AS

EMBROIDERED BURNOUS CLOAKS, CASHMERE SCARFS, SILK AND
GOLD CURTAINS, EMBROIDERED SHOES, CUSHIONS, JEWELRY-
BOXES, ETC., ETC.

Miscellaneous Art Objects and Curiosities

OF MERIT AND VALUE.

BRIC-A-BRAC, COINS, MINERALS, ARMS, ETC., ETC.

THE PROPERTY OF THE MESSRS. LOW; DAVIS COLLAMORE & CO.; AND OTHER
GENTLEMEN OF NEW YORK; AND FRAZAR & CO. OF CHINA.

THE WHOLE TO BE SOLD AT AUCTION BY GEO. A. LEAVITT & CO.,

AT THEIR

SALE ROOMS, CLINTON HALL,

ASTOR PLACE, NEW YORK,

ON

Friday, the 17th inst., at 2½ o'clock p. m.

AND FOLLOWING DAYS (AS INDICATED IN THE CATALOGUE.)

The Sale concluding on Thursday, the 23d.

The Messrs. LEAVITT, Auctioneers.

The Collection will be on Exhibition Tuesday Morning, December 14th, and continue
open to the Public Day and Evening, until Friday, and every Morning thereafter
until the close of the Sale.

CATALOGUE BY WILLIAM H. STROBRIDGE. DECEMBER, 1875.

INTRODUCTION.

Since the sale of the "Oriental Collection" at Clinton Hall in June last, an unusual interest in Lacquers, Enamels, and Porcelains has manifested itself, as well in the neighboring cities of Boston, Philadelphia, and Albany, as here at home. There has appeared to be an earnest demand for the higher qualities of Oriental wares, as well as the fine Porcelains and Majolicas of Europe; and rather in accordance with this demand, than from any other motive, the gentlemen who own the various classes of valuable goods and objects of art assembled together in this Collection, have placed them at the disposal of the public.

Such a variety is not often presented at one sale; and it is simple justice to say, that so many costly, rare, and beautiful objects are still more rarely found in company, unless when grouped together within the walls of a museum.

In these introductory lines our purpose is not to speak of particular objects, but to invite the public to an Exhibition of the whole Collection, where all may be seen at one view or examined in detail.

In the preparation of the Catalogue we have been particularly studious to avoid exaggeration. In the difficult parts we have taken counsel of the wise ; and it is as pleasant to acknowledge our obligations, as it was profitable to receive the friendly services for which they are due.

WILLIAM H. STROBRIDGE.

CLINTON HALL, *December* 8, 1875.

CATALOGUE.

ORIENTAL BRONZES.

A LARGE PROPORTION OF THEM COLLECTED FROM TEMPLES AND ANTIQUE.

1 PAIR of antique candlesticks, of rich, glowing bronze, and very ornamental shape: the form is a tripod mounted on a circular base, above which are handles; reliefs of flowers, birds, and insects, with dragons' heads surmounting the feet; provided with bronze spikes on which to fix the candles. Height, 9½ inches.

2 FINE old vase of rich dark bronze, somewhat broad in contour, and flaring boldly at the top. Decorated before and in the rear with reliefs, of which the front one, representing a pair of dogs under a tree, is undercut very deeply; two small handles; a pattern of low-relief in squares runs around the base, and forms the back-ground to the ornamental designs. Height, 6 inches.

3 RICHLY decorated vase, broad and flaring at the rim; the body of the vessel is divided by deep indentations into four lobes, covered with figures in bas-relief; the neck has flowers and divinities in higher relief, before and behind. Height, 5½ inches.

4 PAIR of beautiful old candlesticks resting on tripods upon a circular base, and ornamented with the inverted lotos flower, above which the stick expands into a globu-

lar form, decorated with bas-reliefs of lotus flowers and leaves, and provided with projecting ornaments in the nature of handles. Height, 8 inches.

5 ELEGANT vase, with flaring rim and rather slender body, decorated with arabesques in relief, of a florid and graceful character; on each side an elephant's head, with pendent ears, whose trunk forms a handle. Height, 7 inches.

6 VASE of tall, slender proportions, almost covered with ornamental patterns in low-relief; the globular swelling in the centre, as well as the foot, is decorated with four projecting stripes, forming a dividing quadrature of the stem. Height, 9 inches.

7 VASE identical in size and style with the last, but with less of the ornamental pattern-work in relief.

8 CANDLESTICK, of tripod form and very decorative design, with dragon curled around the upper part, bas-reliefs on the central portion, and dragons' heads at the insertion of the feet. Height, with spike, 9½ inches.

9 Another, identical in size and general proportions, with minor variations in the ornaments.

10 CYLINDRICAL vase, of simple proportions; the decoration is confined to three belts of ornament, two of them consisting of discs following each other in a row, the third and principal belt decorated with groups of religious symbols in low-relief. Very old and curious. Height, 9¼ inches.

11 ANCIENT vase, oval in section; the general shape is simple but elegant, the ornaments surrounding the vessel in belts are in geometric patterns, made up of circles, squares, etc.; the handles are in the form of two hollow cylinders, an inch in diameter, covered with ornamental patterns, and applied to the slenderest part of the neck. A great curiosity. Height, 11 inches.

12 Another old vase, likewise oval in section, and decorated profusely with dragons and geometric patterns in low-relief. Handles similar to those last described. Height, 7½ inches.

13 Another vase, oval in section, very light and elegant. The swelling portion is decorated with six shield-shaped reliefs, above which are belts of geometric ornament; a pair of slender, branch-like handles springing from rude dragons' heads, descend from near the rim almost to the bottom of the vase ; in front, an inscription in a raised tablet. Height, 9½ inches.

14 Round, broad, urn-shaped vase, in old Japanese bronze, of simple shape, without ornament. On the inside of the rim, which flares to a diameter of seven inches, is an engraved inscription running almost completely around the circumference. A very fine and rare specimen. Made for the Imperial service, bearing the Tycoon's crest. Height, 8 inches.

15 Fine old pair of candlesticks, intended for very large candles, of a pleasing shape, made up of many belts and rings, expanding into a bell shape toward the bottom, and decorated with elephants' heads as handles. Height 22 inches.

16 Candlestick of extremely elegant and graceful design. The socket is shaped like a lotos-flower, which shape occurs again toward the base. A pair of birds in full flight are applied against a central part of the stem, and the lower part is in tripod form. Height, 1 foot.

17 Elegant little candlestick, with tripod base, profusely ornamented. Height, 7½ inches.

18 Curious old vase, square in section, with narrow base and flaring top ; the four sides are alike, and are decorated with a deeply-engraved labyrinthine pattern which occupies the whole surface. Height, 8 inches.

19 Slender vase, of graceful profile, with scalloped rim, a band of ornament round the neck, and slender vines for handles, springing from dragons' heads. Height, 9¼ inches.

20 Similar vase, very old, more slender at the neck, and with scalloped rim ; handles springing from dragons' heads. Height, 8½ inches.

21 Heavy vase, very old, with bulbous body, and three bands
of ornament in low-relief. Height, 8 1-2 inches.

21* Old vase, bulbous body and narrow neck, which is encircled with a band of ornament ; dragon-head handles.
Height, 8½ inches.

22 Old vase, with flaring rim, divided perpendicularly into
4 sections by stripes in relief; almost covered with
pattern-work in low relief. Height, 7¼ inches.

23 Vase, more slender than the last, and with decorations
formed of engraved lines; similar to the above in general features. Height, 7¼ inches.

24 Chinese Brasier, inlaid with silver, resting on tripod
stand decorated with a vine of ivy gilt. It has a lat-
ticed cover, which is also inlaid, and handle similarly
decorated. One of the finest bronzes in the collection.
Dimensions on stand, 8½x10 inches.

25 A Unique Bronze Vessel and Stand, of remarkable form
and great age. It has a spout with faucet of dragon-
shape, and handles of the same design on the sides, the
cover-handle being a buffalo standing at bay. It is
variously decorated with silver inlay representations of
dragons on its plain surface, relief-work inlaid and
chased, and ornaments deeply *incised*. An important
and valuable object. Diameter, 18; height, 21 inches.

26 Pair of small silver inlay Vases, the decorations in high-
relief; old and very fine. Height, 5 inches.   2 pcs

27 Censer to match the vases just described.

28 Old Chinese Plate ; delicate silver inlay work, dragon
subject within inner and outer border. Diameter, 10
inches.

29 Old Chinese Censer, tripod form, with handles ; cover
surmounted by the dog of Fo ; quaint bas-relief decoration. Height, 8 inches.

30 Bronze Buffalo Cow, used as a censer. Cover wanting.

31 Unique and curious fire box, mounted on a branch of the
plum tree, covered with blossoms of beaten silver.
Rare.

32 Old Fire Box of hammered bronze, on tripod support of pine cones; the rim has a beautiful border in the Greek style, and the body is entirely covered with mosaic patterns and Oriental decorations, the maker's name in a cartouche on the bottom. Diameter, 6 in.

33 Chinese Bell, ornamented with curious designs in relief. Height, 7 inches.

34 Pair of small, two-handled Vases, separated into 4 sections by horizontal bars, and elaborately decorated with designs in low-relief; flat, expanded bottoms, and long square necks. Height, about 8 inches.   2 pcs

35 Ancient tripod-candlestick. The design a stalk of bamboo-cane united to a two-handled vase; the whole surmounted by a lotos flower, dragon head, and other decorations. Height, 17 inches.

36 Curious old Candlestick, wanting the nozzle. Height, 16 inches.

37 Pair of Antique Candlesticks, with tripod support on circular base, ornamented with designs in relief; subject, of birds, flowers, dragons' heads, etc. Height, 10 inches.   2 pcs

38 Unique Vase of circular form, elephant handles, oriental figures and scenery; red wood base. Diameter, 10 inches.

39 Statuette of the "Dog of Fo," a spirited work of art. The interior forms a receptacle or vase, of which the head, which is hinged at the collar, is a lifting cover. Greatest diameter, 10 inches.

40 Pair of Bullfrogs, of gigantic size and fine workmanship. Diameter 7 inches.   2 pieces

41 Crab; an admirable representation. Diameter, 1 foot.

42 Bird, on stand of rustic-work; the interior is a hollow receptacle, of which the closed wings form the cover. Height, 9 inches.

43 Aquatic Bird, mounted on a lily-leaf; hollow, with closed wings for cover. Height, 4 inches.

44 Pair of Birds, mounted on rustic work-stand; hollow, with cover formed of the expanded wings and tail. Height, 7 inches.

45 Pair, same. 2 pieces

46 Pair, same. 2 pieces

47 Bird, same. 1 piece

48 Chinese Cup for pouring libations, called Tsio, resembling an inverted helmet, mounted on three feet; dragon handle and band of ornament. Height, 5 inches. Rare.

49 Curious elongated tripod bowl, the form representing a fruit. There are 3 bas-reliefs of religious personages, and an inscription on a square stamp beneath. Diameter, 8 inches.

50 Oblong Fire-Box, on four feet; the rim is encircled with a representation of bamboo; the general surface corrugated with figures of bats and dragon-flies in relief. 7x5½ inches.

51 Hexagonal Bowl, on tripod stand; corrugated surface with dragon-flies in relief. Diameter, 7 inches.

52 Pair of Old Vases, with high, narrow necks and bulbous bodies, one slightly decorated, the other plain. Height, 10 inches. 2 pieces

53 Pair of Antique Vases, on tripod stands, with square handles, expanding at the tops into discs 1 foot in diameter, which can be detached. Height, 12½ inches. 2 pieces

54 Old Vase, expanding at the top into a disc with decorated edge, of 10 inches diameter. Height, 9 inches.

55 Another, almost identical; same general proportion.

56 Pair of Vases, plain and elegant. Height, 7 inches.

57 Pair of Small Vases, of finest workmanship. Handles of birds' heads, and relief of lotos plants, beautifully designed. Height, 4½ inches. 2 pieces

58 Small Jar, of elegant shape, like that of a Greek vase, of finest bronze, with handle and five shield-shaped stamped ornaments. Flawed. Height, 7 inches. Rare.

59 ANCIENT CENSER, tripod form, with dragon handles; cover surmounted by a monster holding a ball; bas-reliefs all around. Height, 4 inches.

60 ANTIQUE, similar, censer on circular base; height, 4 inches.

61 Another, closely similar; height, 4 inches.

62 ANCIENT BOWL, 4 inches in diameter, with top which can be detached, in form of a disc, 1 foot in diameter; the base is a very curious piece of workmanship, being a bold representation of the waves of the sea. Height, 8 inches.

63 ANCIENT BOWL, with zigzag border, and containing a smaller bowl; the base, which can be detached, is similar to last. Diameter, 8¼ inches; height, 6 inches.

64 ANCIENT BOWL, of funnel shape, and containing a smaller bowl like the last; mounted on a base representing a gourd-vine, with leaves and gourds. Diameter, 9 inches.

65 SMALLER BOWL, mounted on a vine. Diameter, 6 inches.

66 FINE OLD VASE, with lid, resting upon a tripod; almost without ornament, except a series of arcades passing around the circumference. Height, 10 inches.

67 VASE, similarly ornamented, with detachable top in form of a disc 10½ inches in diameter, on tripod. Height, 8 inches.

68 PAIR OF DISCS, 11 inches in diameter, with deep cups in the middle, probably the tops of vases, but complete in themselves. 2 pieces

69 GIGANTIC VASE, of high antiquity; cylindrical shape, swelling at the centre into a globe, whereon are handles, consisting of large rings held in the mouths of monsters; the decorations completely cover the vase, and consist of 20 belts of labyrinthine ornament in low-relief. Magnificent specimen. Height, 38 inches.

70 PAIR of splendid Antique Vases, with globular bodies and flaring tops; rims ornamented with rows of discs in relief, and bases with shield-shaped stamps; around the necks are spirited figures of dragons in detached relief, and the bodies are beautifully ornamented with wreaths of flowers, and birds in alto-relievo, relieved with gilding. Height, 26 inches. Fine and rare. 2 p.

71 FINE OLD VASE, elegantly shaped, with dragon handles, and ornaments of labyrinthine pattern around the neck and base. Height, 11 inches.

72 VASE, elegantly proportioned, of plain antique bronze ; the handles ascend in the form of branches from dragons' mouths. Height, 10 inches.

73 FINE ANCIENT VASE, with flaring top and slender neck, on which is a band of labyrinthine ornament, and two dragon handles. Height, 10 inches.

74 RARE VASE, with top expanding into a disc, around whose edge are ornaments of circular beads ; a similar line of decoration surrounds the body, and the neck is covered with wave-like forms. Height, 7 inches ; diameter, 9 inches.

75 SIMILAR VASE, with top expanding to a disc, and figure of a dragon in high-relief around the middle. Height, 6 inches.

76 CURIOUS VASE, of variegated bronze, the lighter portions suggesting an alloy of gold irregularly distributed. The prominent parts are covered with engraved work representing birds. Height, 7½ inches.

77 FINE OLD VASE, with figures of deities in relief on the neck, and beneath, a tree in full blossom in alto-relievo. Height, 5½ inches.

78 VASE, with 4 handles and fanciful patterns in low-relief. Height, 8 inches.

79 ENGRAVED VASE, with ornaments in cartouches, and projecting stripes dividing the body into 4 portions. Height, 6 inches.

80 VASE without handles and engraved ornaments. Height, 6 inches.

81 VASE with dragon handles and ornaments in cartouches. Height, 5½ inches.

82 VASE with dragon handles, reliefs of birds front and rear. Height, 5 inches.

83 VASE with dragon handles, the body decorated with 4 circular reliefs. Height, 5 inches.

84 VASE with dragon handles, decorated with groups of birds. Height, 4 inches.

85 HEXAGONAL Vase, stamped with ornaments in low-relief. Height, 6 inches.

86 RARE and beautiful little vase in imitation of basket-work. Height, 6½ inches.

87 VASE with slender dragon handles, graceful and curious. Height, 7 inches.

88 VASE with scalloped rim, and elephants' heads for handles. Height, 6½ inches.

89 VASE with dragon handles, tortoises in bas-reliefs on the body. Height, 6 inches.

90 VASE with dragon handles. Height, 6 inches.

91 VASE surrounded by the figure of a dragon. Height, 5 inches.

JAPANESE WOOD LACQUERS.

92 GOLD and Black Lacquer Cabinet, silver-mounted; folding doors, six drawers within, and one below. Height, 18 inches; breadth, 15 inches. Fine quality.

93 —— Similar to last, with a slight difference in the decoration. Same dimensions.

94 NEST of Gold and Black Lacquer Boxes, silver-mounted, with locks and keys; ornamented with chrysanthemums and birds; largest 10x16 inches. Fine quality.
                                                                    3 p

95 —— Repetition of last.   3 p

96 NEST of Gold and Brown Lacquer Trays, two in a set, ornamented with squirrels and grape-vines. Square, with rounded corners, 20x20 inches.   2 p

97 —— Similar to last, decorated with poultry subjects. Same size.   2 p

98 SQUARE Black Lacquer Tray, with a mysterious Japanese inscription in gold; containing a set of four small black and gold lacquer boxes, each in shape of a fan, the four forming a circle.   5 p

99 Tray similar to last, but uninscribed; containing four small black and gold lacquer boxes, of various and ingenious shapes, such as shells, cinquefoils, etc.   5 p

100 —— Repetition of last.   5 p

101 Black and gold lacquer revolving top centre-table; embossed with the figure of a peacock; diameter, 27 inches.

102 Similar to last; embossed with falcon and sparrow.

103 Oblong Tray, diameter 20 inches, of a rich black engraved lacquer, being the Japanese style corresponding with the rare Chinese Sou-chou lacquer. Ornamented with the "peach of longevity."

104 Another, same size, different ornament.

105 Pressed cinnabar lacquer box, 12x14 inches, containing six card-boxes in black and gold lacquer.

106 Similar to last, black lacquer, same size.

107 Miniature cabinet, black and gold lacquer, on stand, silver-mounted, folding doors; box on top with lifting cover.

108 Similar to last, aventurine lacquer.

109 Tray and contents, like No. 99.   .   5 p

110 Another, same in all respects.   5 p

111 Nest of brown and gold lacquer trays, 12x20 inches, convolvulus ornament.   2 p

112 Similar nest, black and gold lacquer.   2 p

113 Similar nest, black and gold lacquer, somewhat smaller.
      2 p

114 Repetition of last.   2 p

115 Nest, oval, black and gold lacquer, diameter, 14 inches.
      2 p

116 Nest, repetition of last.   2 p

117 Nest of gold and black lacquer boxes, silver-mounted, with locks and keys; embossed ornaments of peonies and butterflies. Fine quality.   3 p

118 Repetition of last.   3 p

119 Cigar-Box, black and gold lacquer, pierced for four and a half-dozen cigars, with lock and key. Inlaid with ivory and pearl; 8x11 inches.

120 Another, same in all respects.

121 CIRCULAR black and gold lacquer Joss-House, in four compartments; two, gold lined, with idols erect, two fitted as cigar holders; handsomely decorated. Height, 12 inches.

122 Similar to last.

122* BLACK lacquer card-box, embossed with birds, etc., in gold and colors; containing boxes for 6 packs, and secret drawers. Size 10x12 inches.

123 Repetition of last.

124 Another, precisely similar.

125 SIMILAR, silver-mounted, 4 boxes inside and drawer below, handsome decorations. 8x10 inches.

126 Repetition of last.

127 Another, same in all respects.

128 BLACK and gold lacquer paper box, with paper-press or follower. 8x10 inches.

129 Another.

130 Another.

131 Another.

132 PAIR Miniature Cabinets in black and gold lacquer, handle on top. The sliding front reveals 3 silver-mounted drawers. Height, 7 inches.   2 pcs

133 Another pair, same in every respect.   2 pcs

134 PAIR black and gold lacquer boxes, with lifting covers, silver-mounted, lock and key; containing two decorated boxes with sliding covers.   2 pcs

135 Repetition of last.   2 pcs

136 PAIR of silver-mounted gold and black lacquer miniature cabinets, with lock and key, handle on top; containing three drawers. 6x7 inches.   2 pcs

137 Repetition of last.   2 pcs

138 PAIR of black pressed lacquer boxes, with trays inside. 5x7 inches.   2 pcs

139 Same as last.   2 pcs

140 Another pair, same as last.   2 pcs

141 NEST of brown lacquer trays, square, with rounded corners, decorated with gold and colors. 18x18 inches.
                2 pcs

142 Same, oblong.   12x18 inches.   2 pcs
143 Repetition of last.   2 pcs
144 Same; also oblong, red lacquer.   10x15 inches.   2 pcs
145 Repetition of last.   2 pcs
146 NEST of black-lacquer trays, square, with rounded cor-
    ners, decorated with peacocks and flowers.   18x18
    inches.   2 pcs
147 Same, oblong.   12x18 inches.   2 pcs
148 Repetition of last.   2 pcs
149 Same, also oblong.   10x15.   2 pcs
150 Repetition of last.   2 pcs
151 NEST of square black and aventurine lacquer trays, dec-
    orated.   11x11 inches.   2 pcs
152 Repetition of last.   2 pcs
153 NEST of circular black and gold lacquer trays, orna-
    mented.   Diameter, 9 inches.   2 pcs
154 SQUARE black lacquer tray, on feet, and contents, viz.,
    four fancy boxes.   5 pcs
155 Repetition of last.   5 pcs
156 Similar tray, and contents, 10 hexagonal (honeycomb)
    boxes, all handsomely decorated.   11 pcs

JAPANESE PORCELAIN AND POTTERY.

157 PAIR porcelain vases, ovoid form, flaring at the tops,
    with scalloped rims, decorated both inside and out
    with flowers and figures in brilliant colors.   Height,
    30 inches.   2 pcs
158 PAIR similar vases, same form.   Height, 36 inches.   2 pcs
159 Another pair, same as last.   One mended.   2 pcs
160 Similar pair.   Height, 32 inches.   2 pcs
161 PAIR fine cylinder-shaped Japanese vases, decorated with
    human figures, flowers, and insects in gold and colors.
    Masks for handles.   2 pcs
162 PAIR blue vases, ovoid form, flaring at the top, scalloped
    rims, decorated with large figures of turkey and pheas-
    ant; a section at the base lacquered.   Height, 48
    inches.   2 pcs

163 Pair similar vases, same color and decoration. Height, 36 inches. 2 pcs

164 Pair vases, ovoid form, flaring at the top, with scalloped rims, decorated with flowers and figures inside and out, brilliant colors on white ground. Height, 36 inches. 2 p

165 Pair similar vases, with narrow vine painted on the edges, variegated decorations on white ground. Height, 36 inches. 2 p

166 Pair similar vases, scalloped rims, same decorations. Height, 30 inches. 2 p

167 Pair similar vases, plain round tops, slightly flaring; spreading at base, and tastefully decorated in various colors on white ground. Height, 30 inches. 2 p

168 Pair similar vases, ovoid form, boldly flaring tops with crinkled edges, variegated decoration. Height, 30 inches. 2 p

169 Pair slender vases, of tasteful form, narrow cylindrical necks intersected by a band; beautifully decorated with figures in medallions and other ornaments. Height, 30 inches. 2 p

170 Pair similar vases, with red and gold necks circumscribed by a band, variegated decorations on white. 24 inches. 2 p

171 Another pair, same in all respects. 2 p

172 Pair similarly decorated, with elegant paintings of flowers and birds. Height, 24 inches. 2 p

173 Another pair, similar to last, with figure in cartouches. Height, 24 inches. 2 p

174 Pair vases, high ovoid form, with cylindrical necks and plain tops, decorated in brilliant colors. Height, 24 inches. 2 p

175 Superb pair of enameled and lacquered porcelain vases, with panels of embossed ornaments, in gold and colors, on red and black grounds. Height, 18 inches. 2 p

176 Pair of fine crackle vases, high ovoid form, enameled with birds, chrysanthemums and other flowers, trees, etc., in natural colors on gray ground; red and gold tops. Fine. Height, 13 inches.   2 p

177 Pair, similar.   2 p

178 Pair gray crackle vases, slightly flaring at base and top, ornaments in medallions and panels. Rare. Height, 12 inches.   2 p

179 Pair white crackle vases, flaring scalloped tops, and slightly spreading bottoms, contracted at the base; richly decorated in bright colors, red and gold borders. Height, 13 inches.   2 p

180 Pair bottle-shaped vases, long necks, spreading tops decorated with chain border on the edges, and variegated ornaments. Height, 13 inches.   2 p

181 Another pair, similar. Height, 11 inches.   2 p

182 Repetition of last.   2 p

183 Another pair, same in all respects.   2 p

184 Pair vases, high, nearly cylindrical form, short necks and spreading tops, red rims, enameled in gold and colors. Height, 12 inches.   2 p

185 Another pair, identical in all respects.   2 p

186 Similar pair, the rim of one broken.   2 p

187 Pair of cylindrical form vases, with narrow necks, decorated with large flies for handles; painted vertical rim and red spreading base; enameled with figures, etc.; very fine. Height, 14 ins.   2 p

188 Pair, duplicate of last.   2 p

189 Pair vases, high ovoid form, with narrow necks and scalloped tops, variegated decorations in panels on white ground. Height, 14 ins.   2 p

190 Pair vases, repetition of last; one slightly mended.   2 p

191 Pair of vases, slightly ovoid in form, with wide, short necks decorated with band of gold and red, which is repeated at the base; enameled with figures of golden pheasants. Height, 13 ins.   2 p

192 Kaga bowl, large size, decorated on all sides with landscapes and figures in red and gold. Diameter, 9 ins.

193 Similar, same colors, different decorations. Diameter, 9 ins.

194 Another, similar in size and decoration.

195 KIOTO tea-pot, high fluted pattern, twisted handle, painted with chrysanthemums and wild-flowers in colors. Height, 10 ins.

196 Another, precisely similar.

197 One of flat canteen shape, pine-tree decoration.

198 Another, canteen shape, smaller.

199 One low pattern, square form, decorated in the paste with figures of storks and flowers, and painted in colors.

200 Another, similar.

201 Another, similar.

202 Another, similar.

203 Another, similar.

204 Another, similar.

205 Another, similar.

206 Another, similar.

207 Another, similar.

208 Another, similar.

209 Another, similar.

210 Another, similar.

211 Another, similar.

212 PORCELAIN tea-pot, low pattern, decorations in cobalt blue on pure white ground, socket handle.

213 PORCELAIN cigar-box, with cover; cylindrical form, oriental figures in bright colors on white ground.

213*a* Same.

213*b* Same.

213*c* Same.

ORIENTAL WOOD LACQUERS.

214 SQUARE black lacquer tray and contents, viz., four fancy
boxes, various shapes.   5 p

215 NESTS of 2 red lacquer trays, and 6 red-lined lacquer
bowls, of which the external one has a cover. Curious
and fine.   8 p

216 Same.   8 p
217 Same.   8 p
218 Same.   8 p
219 Same.   8 p
220 Same.   8 p

221 NESTS of ornamented lacquer-ware, consisting of 2 oval
trays, 2 covered boxes, with knobs, and 3 scalloped
bowls.   7 p

222 Same.   7 p
223 Same.   7 p
224 Same.   7 p
225 Same.   7 p
226 Same.   7 p

227 SELECTION of choice objects in ornamented lacquer in
nests, viz., 2 circular trays, 5 saki bowls, 3 covered
boxes, and nest of 6 eggs, separately decorated and
very curious.   16 p

228 Same.   16 p
229 Same.   16 p
230 Same.   16 p
231 Same.   16 p
232 Same.   16 p
233 Same.   16 p
234 Same.   16 p

235 NEST of 3 best quality vermilion lacquer saki cups, with lining of gold lacquer, embossed with exquisite decorative figures. 3 p

235a NEST of 3 similar cups, differently decorated. 3 p

235b Similar nest. 3 p

236 CIRCULAR centre-table, with revolving top, in gold and black lacquer, beautifully embossed ornament of golden pheasant, etc., natural size. Diameter. 28 ins.

237 Similar to last, embossed with pair of pheasants. Same size.

238 NEST of fine quality gold and black lacquer boxes, silver-mounted, with locks and keys; embossed with floral ornaments in gold and colors. Largest, 16x10 ins.
3 p

239 Repetition of last. 3 p

240 Repetition of last. 3 p

241 SILVER-mounted gold and black lacquer cabinet, with folding doors; large drawer below and six inside, 18 ins. high by 15 ins. breadth; excellent quality.

242 Repetition of last.

243 PRESSED cinnabar lacquer box of octagon shape, with panel of gold and black lacquer in cover; 7½ inches diameter.

244 Similar box, in black pressed lacquer.

245 Similar oblong box, same material as last; 7½ inches diameter.

246 Another.

247 PAIR OF MINIATURE CABINETS, in gold and black lacquer, with handle on top. Sliding front, behind which are 3 silver-mounted drawers; height, 7 inches. 2 pieces

248 Another pair; same as last. 2 pieces

249 DAIMIO CABINET, with handle on top; black and gold lacquer, ornamented with crests; silver-mounted door, revealing three drawers. Fine.

250 Similar cabinet, with different decorations.

251 Another, with daimio crests.

252 Similar to last, with different ornaments.

2

253 Pair of gold and black lacquer boxes, with lifting cover, silver-mounted, with lock and key, containing two decorated boxes with sliding lids.   2 pieces

254 Another pair, repetition of last.   2 pieces

255 Fine gold and black lacquer box, silver-mounted, with lock and key; decorated with chrysanthemums and birds. Containing 2 similar boxes, one fitting within the other.   3 pieces

256 Fine Card-box, in black lacquer, with embossed decorations in gold and colors; containing boxes for 6 packs, and magic drawers. 10x12 inches.

258 Repetition of last.

259 Cigar-box, black and gold lacquer, pierced for four and a half dozen cigars, with lock and key; lid inlaid with ivory and pearl. 8x11 inches.

260 Another, same size.

261 Another, similar in all respects.

262 Another, repetition of last.

263 Pair black and gold lacquer papeteries, with paper-press or follower. 8x10 inches; covers inlaid with pearl and shells.   2 pieces

264 Another pair, similar to last.   2 pieces

265 Another pair, slightly different in decoration.   2 pieces

266 Another pair, similar.   2 pieces

267 Pair of gold and black lacquer boxes, silver-mounted, with lock and key; each with tray, containing 2 aventurine lacquer card boxes. 6½x8½ inches.
      2 pieces

268 Another pair, same.   2 pieces

269 Another pair, same.   2 pieces

270 Another pair, same.   2 pieces

271 Another pair, same.   2 pieces

272 Aventurine-lacquer Centre-table, with falling top, finely decorated with gold figures on black ground. Diameter, 2 feet.

273 Similar to last.

274 Nest of rich brown lacquer trays, square, with rounded corners, decorated in gold and colors.   2 pieces

275 Same.   2 pieces

276 Same.   2 pieces

277 Same, black lacquer, with gold and colors.   2 pieces
278 Same as last.   2 pieces
279 Same.   2 pieces
280 OBLONG TRAY, of a rare black engraved lacquer, decorated with curious mythological subject, dragon, and water-fall. 16x20 inches.
281 Companion.
282 NEST fine brown lacquer trays, richly embossed with landscape subjects in gold and colors. 12x20 inches.
   2 pieces
283 Similar to last.   2 pieces
284 Similar to last.   2 pieces
285 Same, in black lacquer, with gold and colors.   2 pieces
286 Same.   2 pieces
287 Same.   2 pieces
288 Similar, 12x18 inches.   2 pieces
289 Same as last.   2 pieces
290 Same as last.   2 pieces
291 NEST red lacquer Trays, decorated. 9x15 inches.
   2 pieces
292 Same.   2 pieces
293 Same.   2 pieces
294 Same, with three nests of lacquer boxes.   10 pieces
295 Same.   10 pieces
296 Same.   10 pieces
297 Same.   10 pieces
298 Same.   10 pieces
299 Same, with nest of (3) scalloped bowls; ditto, of (6) saki bowls, with red lining, the outer one with cover, and telescope work-box. All choice.   12 pieces
301 Same.   12 pieces
302 Same.   12 pieces
303 Same.   12 p
304 Same.   12 p
305 Same, with red saki-bowl, cigar-case, and 4 covered boxes.
   8 p
306 Same.   8 p
307 Same.   8 p
308 Same.   8 p
309 Same.   8 p

310 Circular Joss-house, gold and black lacquer, in 4 compartments, 2 with gold lining, in which are carved idols;
the other two fitted up as cigar-boxes. Height, 12 ins.

311 Duplicate.

312 Gold and Black Lacquer Cabinet, silver mounted, with
folding doors; one large and six small drawers, handsomely decorated. Height 19 ins. and breadth 14 ins.

313 Another, similar; same size.

314 Small Cabinet, black and gold lacquer, on stand; silver-
mounted, with folding doors; box on top, with lifting
cover. Height, 15 ins.

315 Similar to last; aventurine lacquer.

316 Pressed black lacquer box, with birds in relief on the
cover; 12x14 ins., containing six card-boxes in black
and gold lacquer.

317 Similar to last; aventurine lacquer, embossed with a falcon in gold and colors; contents the same.

318 Cinnabar lacquer box, octagonal form, cover decorated
with embossed figures on black ground. Diameter,
7½ ins.

319 Same.

320 Same.

321 Same.

322 Nest of tea-caddies, square form, of silver and black
diced lacquer, each box having two covers, of which the
outer one is handsomely ornamented in gold and black.
Height of largest, 7 ins.   3 p

323 Same.   3 p
324 Same.   3 p
325 Same.   3 p
326 Same.   3 p
327 Same.   3 p

328 Nest of three (3) best quality vermilion lacquer saki-cups,
lined with gold lacquer, embossed with exquisite decorations of insects, flowers, etc.   3 p

329 Same.   3 p

330 DAIMIO Cabinet in black and gold lacquer, decorated with crests; silver-mounted; handle on top; lock and key to door, which when opened reveals three drawers. Fine.

331 Similar, with slightly different ornament.

332 Similar to last.

333 Similar to last.

334 Similar to last.

335 Similar to last.

336 MINIATURE Cabinet, in gold and black lacquer, with handle on top; sliding front, behind which are three silver-mounted drawers. Height, 7 ins.

337 Same.

338 Same.

339 Same.

340 Same.

341 Same.

342 HANDKERCHIEF-BOX, in fine black lacquer, inlaid with coral and ivory, and embossed with metallic colors. The decoration is a fine example of Japanese taste.

343 Same.

344 Same.

345 Same.

346 Same.

347 FINE work-box in black lacquer, inlaid with ivory, coral, and mother-of-pearl ornaments; silver-mounted, with lock and key. Size 9x12 ins.

348 Same.

349 Same.

350 Same.

351 Same.·

352 Same.

353 FINE gold and black lacquer work-box, with lifting tray, containing six small decorated boxes; at the bottom a drawer which slides in four directions. The decorations are rich and abundant on five sides. Size, 9½x12 ins.

354 Same.

355 Same.

356 Same.

357 Same.

358 Same.

VARIOUS.

358*a* OLD Chinese enamel bowl decorated with borders and shrubs on the outside; the inside ornamented with borders and net-work of scales, and on the bottom a fish subject; a piece of the oldest and best cloisonné. Diameter, 9 ins.

[On black-wood stand.]

358*b* A BOWL of the same age and quality, with different decorations. Same size.

[Also on stand.]

358*c* NEST of five Foo-Chow lacquer boxes, each box with peculiar decorations. Size 4½x4. 5 p

[This Foo-Chow lacquer is rare to excess even in China, and is only to be obtained of a single family who possess the secret of its composition. The present example is extremely beautiful, quite unlike anything before seen by the writer.]

358*d* Foo-Chow lacquer box, with fine gilt handles and mountings, decorated with representations of the coins of different emperors' reigns to the number of twenty-seven; lining aventurine lacquer; unique and valuable. About 12x16 ins.

358*e* LARGE Japanese circular tray, with thick escalloped rim of aventurine lacquer; the bottom black with squares of fine gold embossed lacquer decorations; vermilion lacquer back. Rare and fine. Diameter about 18 ins.

358*f* CIRCULAR silk-embroidered screen, birds and flowers on white, mounted in black-wood frame handsomely carved.

358*g* FINE gold and black lacquer box; subject of decoration, storks under a plum-tree in blossom. About 7x9 ins.

359 SOU-CHOU cinnabar lacquer bowl, in two colors, elaborately carved with Chinese figures and scenery. An inscription on the bottom defines its age as between three and four hundred years. Diameter, 7½ inches.

360 SET of 32 chess-men in ivory, elaborately and magnificently carved by a Chinese artist, the large pieces five inches in height.

361 IVORY ball, with 17 concentric shells, each carved with marvellous skill. Slight fracture on the outer shell. Diameter, over 4 inches.

[Balls of this size and number of shells are rare and expensive.]

362 GOLD-MOUNTED sword, with richly garnished scabbard of the finest aventurine lacquer, decorated with a daimio's crest of three open fans in a circle, which is repeated on the mountings and hilt.

[This was the court-sword of Prince Aidzu, one of the most brave and powerful Daimios who adhered to the Tycoon, in opposition to the Mikado. The writer has in his possession an interesting account of his career, culminating in the Tycoon's surrender at Yeddo.]

363 DAIMIO's sword, with finest lacquer scabbard, shark-skin hilt wound with white silk, and decorated with crests. The blade damascened. *Valuable.*

364 Similar sword, the hilt wound with black silk.

365 LOUIS XVI. service of Bohemian glass on or-moulu stand, with plate-glass mirror in the bottom. The pieces are: a decanter, *carafon*, goblet, and sugar-bowl, each magnificently embossed in gold and colors. From the Dekon sale, Boston, 1871.

366 PORCELAIN vase, period of the First Empire, of classical form, with mask handles. Panels handsomely painted with animals on gold ground. Height, 11 inches.

367 SUPERB porcelain vase, almost covered with applied flower-work in high-relief, modeled and painted in the colors of nature; rustic handles, gilt, running to the base. Painted with Persian subjects, whose costumes are ornamented with jewels in relief, and which are equally elaborate on each side of the vase. Height, 18 inches.

368 SEVRES teacup and saucer, gold lining and bands, green-enameled body, with flowers in festoons. Mark— "Sèvres," under a crown.

369 HIGHLAND belt pistol, silver-mounted, " Alexander Cambell " engraved on it. Obtained from a descendant of Rob Roy Macgregor. Very fine and valuable.

370 Pair Wedgewood green jasper plaques; subject, Vestal Virgins, in white. 2 p

371 Pair fine Japanese bronze vases, tripod supports, decorated with dragon subjects in high-relief. Inscription stamped on the bottom. Height, 12 inches. 2 p

372 Old Japanese two-handled vase, tripod form, expanding at the top into a shallow basin which can be removed. The body of the vase decorated with fish and stork in high-relief. Height, 12 inches.

373 Bronze thermometer, Fahrenheit, in form of a terminal bust of Schiller.

374 Florentine bronze statuette, a mechanical reproduction of the antique statue, "Boy Extracting a Thorn." Very fine.

375 Pair of magnificent two-handled vases on circular stands. with spreading tops in the form of receivers; the bodies are cylindrical, with flattened sides. Ornaments of vines, flowers, insects, and birds in silver inlay work, with embossing in shakdo, cover almost the entire exterior surface. Height, 12½ inches. 2 p

376 Old Delft Plaque, painted in blue, with the Judgment of Solomon; the form is square-oblong, with thick marbled rim to represent a frame; there is an inscription in a cartouch, and date on the back—IKON-INGEN, 3v23—1678; it has been broken and carefully mended. A remarkable and rare piece of pottery. 12x16.

377 One of different form, shield-shape, with scroll border painted in bright colors. Subject: Venus attended by Cupid; painted in blue; mended. 11x15 inches.

378 Mammoth Bowl; Japanese porcelain, decorated with Oriental figures and foliage in bright enamel colors; the back painted in blue. Diameter, 27 inches.

379 Another, same dimensions, similar.

379* Pair of these immense bowls, same as those described.
2 p

380 CARD Receiver. Steatite, leaf-shape. 8x9 inches.

381 Similar.

382 Similar.

383 —— Square form.

384 Similar.

385 SUPERB bronze statuette, by Aimé Millet, of Paris. Subject, Ariadne weeping at finding herself deserted by Theseus on the island of Naxos. Exquisitely modeled and finished.

386 BOX of 10 Chinese Puzzles, elaborately carved in ivory. Sold as one lot.

387 JAPANESE hand-mirror, fine etched back. About 8 inches diameter. In case.

388 DOUBLE hand-mirror, French, richly enameled and jeweled.

389 BOULE box, containing the game of "Boston." French workmanship.

390 COLUMN of Marcus Aurelius, in Rosso-Antico, from the original at Rome; black marble base. Height, 26 in.

391 PAIR handsome Japanese porcelain vases, decorated with ornaments in large and small medallions in gold and colors on vermilion ground. Height, 12 inches. 2 p

392 Another pair, similar.

393 HALF-dozen finest Japanese egg-shell porcelain covered cups and saucers, decorated with figures in blue medallions on red and gold ground. (18, sold as) 6 p

394 HALF-dozen cups and saucers, repetition of last. 6 p

395 HALF-dozen cups and saucers, repetition of last. 6 p

396 FINEST Japanese enameled porcelain coffee-pot, completely covered with panel and chrysanthemum decorations in brilliant colors. Height, 11 inches.

397 Similar coffee-pot in pure white porcelain, enameled with trees and flowers in gold and natural colors. Height, 11 inches.

398 CHOCOLATE-pot, long pattern, similar decorations.

399 PAIR Kioto vases, oviform body, short neck; spreading at top and base, decorated with beautiful drawings of natural flowers in gold and colors. One mended. Height, 12 inches. 2 p

400 Kioto tea-pot, large size, with bamboo handle; decoration similar to last. Extremely fine.

401 —— Tea-pot, repetition of last.

402 Kioto wine-pot, high cylindrical form, quaint decorations of insects and foliage, admirably drawn and colored. Height, 8 inches.

403 Wine-pot, similar to last.

404 Another, high ovoid form, decorations of birds and foliage. Height, 8 inches.

405 Another, similar.

406 Another, similar, somewhat smaller.

407 Another, with flanged and fluted bottom. Height, 7 in.

408 Kioto tea-pot, globular form, bamboo handle, finely decorated with birds and flowers. Height, 8 inches.

409 Another, similar decorations, same size.

409* Another, similar form. Height, 7 inches.

410 Another, fluted hexagonal form, painted with birds and flowers.

411 Another, fluted and flanged at the bottom, with wire-wrapped handles. Height, 7 inches.   ‘

412 Another, same shape, etc. Height, 7 inches.

413 Small globular tea-pot, beautifully decorated.

414 Pair large Kioto flower-pots, tripod base, decorated with birds and flowers. Diameter, 10½ inches.   2 p

415 Similar pair. Diameter, 9 inches.   2 p

416 Similar pair. Diameter, 7½ inches.   2 p

417 Similar pair. Diameter, 6 inches.   2 p

418 Pair flower-pots, Kioto porcelain, rich decorations on white ground ; red rims. Diameter, 6 inches.   2 p

419 Pair flower-pots, same as last.   2 p

OLD PORCELAIN AND POTTERY.

ORIENTAL.

[Although sensible people may sometimes thoughtlessly ridicule the passion of the curious for old china, a little reflection will convince them of their folly.

So far from being an idle or frivolous fancy, the desire to possess rare and remarkable examples of the potter's skill is to be commended upon every ground on which we extol the patronage of art. It is a taste that has manifested itself among the cultivated of every age and race, and the love for graceful forms and agreeable colors that so strongly marks the human mind, has nowhere found more satisfying objects than here.

The highest genius and the best skill of man have been employed in the production of pottery, and it is only reasonable that our esteem for what is best in the works of the present or past should be accordingly great. Let those who open their eyes with astonishment at the prices paid for old porcelain or painted earthenware, learn that the pieces sought for by amateurs are *works of art*, and were valued as such at the time of their production. They have never been *cheap* in the popular sense, and they are not *dear* now at the prices they command.]

420 SMALL Nef or table ornament of white porcelain, decorated with blue. It is of octagon form with reticulated sides. Very fine.

421 SATSUMA Fire Box, in a double form, the smaller box serving as a cover for the larger, which has gored and pierced sides, with two inverted shell handles, and four feet; the whole is covered with a fine crackle glaze, and decorated with pines, foliage, and fruit, in blue, green, and gold. Extremely fine and valuable. Height, 10 inches.

422 JAPANESE Porcelain Fire-box, on stand; enameled with blue, green, and red colors, with cloisonne patterns, worked in gold; reticulated cover. Diameter, 8 inches.

423 Saki Bottle of old Satsuma, crackle; the form is octagon, with decorations in blue, green, and gold; extremely fine. Height, 7 inches.

424 Tea-Caddy, pottery; it has an uneven surface showing finger marks methodically arranged under a variegated transparent glaze, decorated with butterflies and flowers in relief, in brilliant enamel colors. Height, 9 inches.

425 Water Jar, bucket form, with handle on top between two red wings; the whole surface beautifully enameled in the style of mosaic work; the ground a fine and rare yellow. Height, 10 inches.

426 Crackle Porcelain Vase, with a rich lustrous and variegated glaze of many colors; spreading top; very rare. Height, 12 inches.

427 Another Smaller Vase of variegated colors in the glaze; ovoid form; two masks in the place of handles, on black-wood stand. Height of all, 8 inches.

428 Engraved Celadon Vase, sea-green color; high ovoid form; small neck with bronze collar; the subjects of the decorations are arabesques and flowers incised in the body of the vase; the glaze is highly translucent and the tone agreeable. Very rare. Height, 14 inches.

429 Jardinier, square form, on 4 feet, springing from lions' heads; decoration in panels, dragon subject in light blue; porcelain. Height, 10 inches.

430 Sanpan Dish (boat) of blue and white porcelain. Length, 11½ inches.

431 Another Large Dish in the form of a batteau; blue decorations, with a celadon glaze on the inside. Length, 15 inches.

432 Old Circular Plaque; ultra-marine blue, with yellow edge. Diameter, 17 inches.

433 Old Japanese Idol; red stone ware; seated figure holding a grape leaf; very finely modeled. Height 11 inches.

434 Group, cock and hen, of similar ware; the execution extremely fine. Height, 11 inches.

435 PAIR of Fruit Baskets, reticulated sides and painted borders ; fine example of this kind of open work ; wanting the handles. 2 p

436 PLATE, of oval shape, to match last. 7x9 inches.

GERMAN.

DELFT.

437 HOLLAND Delft Plates, painted with flowers and foliage, in blue, yellow rim ; quaint. Diameter, 9 inches. 6 p

438 OTHERS ; same style, different pattern. 9 inches. 3 p

439 PLATE, on which the Story of the Prodigal Son is illustrated by three figures at a gaming table. DEN. VERLOO REN. ZOON ; the border scalloped and painted with a band of foliage and flowers in high colors. Diameter, 10 inches.

440 PLATE, decorated with a lily and butterflies ; narrow rim; old Holland. 9 inches. 2 p

441 PLATE, thick bottom ; flower basket and border in dark blue. 9 inches.

442 Another ; Flower Vase, with two birds within double border of dark blue. B P F on back. 9 inches.

443 Similar (blue delft) ; yellow edge. 9 inches.

444 BASIN ; round, shallow dish, with yellow, purple, and green decorations ; subject, landscape, within two narrow borders. 11 inches.

445 Similar to last ; different pattern, same size.

446 PLATEAU ; painted with flower basket, within broad border, covering the rim and hanging over in festoons to the bottom ; pale blue. Diameter, 14 inches.

447 Similar ; landscape subject ; narrow border. Same size.

448 ONE with broader rim ; Venus on the Zuy-der-Zee sailing in a cockle-shell. Diameter, 14 inches.

450 DEEP blue Plaque ; quaint decorations ; on back, L. P. K. Diameter, 12 inches.

451 Similar; deeper form; rim slightly scalloped. Diameter, 14 inches.

452 One of the dark blue family, with plain rim. Same size.

453 Another; similar, but deeper form, also with more of the white ground showing through the decorations. Diameter, 14 inches.

454 Plateau; light blue; wide rim divided into 9 sections (volutes); landscape, with figures. Diameter, 14 inches.

455 Similar; broad rim, gored with lines radiating outwards. Diameter, 14 inches.

456 Old pink and blue Plaque, with A. R. in monogram under a crown on the bottom; on the under side, N., for *Niderville.* Diameter, 12 inches.

457 Similar; blue and white, decorated with basket of flowers and birds. Same size.

458 Platter; long octagon, blue and white, painted in the Oriental style. 12x16 inches.

459 Deep blue covered vase, high ovoid form, with sides slightly gored, spreading bottom, decorations of a floral character covering every part. Height, 11 inches.

460 Smaller vase of similar character. Height, 7 inches.

461 Vase of this description of extremely fine quality, with decorations of birds and flowers in large panels; delicious blue and white. Height, 15 inches.

462 Another remarkable vase with long bulbous neck, blue decorations of grotesque figure subject. Slightly nicked at top. Height, 16 inches.

463 Blue and white Delft beer mug, ovoid form, with block-tin cover and bottom rim. 8 inches.

464 Fine Delft beer mug, cylindrical form, block-tin cover and bottom; floral decorations in panels on sprinkled ground. M. S. F. II., 1743, engraved on cover. Height, 9 inches.

465 One with subject of Cavalier, with sword striking backward. 7 inches.

466 Another beer mug of the cylinder shape; 1815 engraved on cover; decoration, bird on garnished shield. 8 inches.

467 BEER Jug, with Brittannia cover and bottom rim; on cover, medallion of George II., King of England. Fine green lustrous glaze; rare. Height, 11 inches.

[Perhaps of English manufacture.]

468 BOQUETIERE blue Delft, with five mouths. Extremely fine and rare.

469 VERY fine two-handled vase, slightly oviform body, short neck, with flange on top; painted in blue with large roses and circle of vines on pink tinted ground. Height, 12 inches.

470 PAIR of Holland Delft vases, hexagonal shape, painted in blue with turretted church and landscape. Height, 12½ inches.

471 ANOTHER of flattened oval shape, painted in blue with river and landscape; by G. Brower, 1764. Height, 11½ inches.

FLEMISH STONE-WARE.

472 BEER Mug, with cover of block-tin, bearing the date 1777. Stone ware. Height, 7 inches.

473 One of the same description, dated 1723.

474 Another with cover and rim on bottom; no date. Very fine.

475 One without cover. 6½ inches.

DRESDEN PORCELAIN.

476 SUPERB platter, painted with a bouquet of flowers in their natural colors, showing with fine effect on the pure white ground; the rim is gold edged, and is encircled by a band of transparent cobalt blue with gold edges. Size 15x20 inches.

477 PLATEAU of circular form maked with S. in the Angle of the crossed swords. It is painted with flowers and butterflies in blue. An extremely fine piece, although it has a slight notch in the rim. Diameter, 15 inches.

478 MARCOLINI Platter, scalloped rim, oval form, fancifully decorated with flowers, one resembling a bird on the wing; the ground a pure white. 13x16 inches.

479 BOWL to match last. It has a border on the inside, of
    red and pale green colors. Diameter, 6½ inches.

480 BASIN with the same decorations. 7 inches.

481 TEA-POT, painted in the same style. Height, 5 inches.

482 COFFEE CUPS and Saucers, to match last; half-dozen of
    each.   6 p

483 Others of same set. One handle mended.   3 p

484 TEA-Cups and saucers (same set), 5 of each.   5 p

485 PLATE of the King's time, signed with the mark of that
    period; narrow scalloped rim, beautifully decorated
    with gold and blue enamel in sections, with flowers be-
    tween, the pattern falling into the bottom, which is
    painted with a flower subject; a border of vines and
    foliage on the back. Diameter, 9¼ inches. Very fine
    and rare.

486 MARCOLINI Plate, gold rim, purple, blue, and green bor-
    der of flowers; birds and butterflies in bright colors on
    the bottom. 9½ inches.

487 PLATE of the King's period. Scalloped rim, light decora-
    tions of flowers. 9½ inches.

488 One with the same mark (dot between the sword hilt)
    the rim and body traversed by vertical curved lines
    raised; chrysanthemums, roses, and other flowers
    painted in bright colors. Deep form; diameter, 9½
    inches.

489 PLATES of the time of Marcolini; gold rim, a bunch of
    flowers exquisitely pencilled in the bottom; deep form
    9 inches.   2 p

490 MARCOLINI dinner plates, the rim edged with yellow;
    small wild flowers in their natural colors pencilled on
    the white ground. Diameter, 9½ inches.   6 p

491 MARCOLINI bowl, similarly decorated, but with the addi-
    tion of larger flowers (lilies) on the outside. Diameter,
    7 inches.

492 COFFEE-POT to match preceding; high pattern; round
    form expanding to the top. Height, 10 inches.

493 TEA-POT, low pattern; same set. Height, 6 inches.

494 MILK-PITCHER, high pattern; same set. Height, 7 ins.

495 Sugar-bowl, expanding to the top; no handles; same set. Height, 6 ins.

496 Tea-cups and saucers; same (six of each).   6 p

497 Same repeated.   6 p

498 Soup-Tureen of the king's period, the surface traversed by raised vertical lines, continued on the cover to the apex, which is surmounted by a child with basket of flowers and fruit; white porcelain decorated with flowers in colors; handles and rim of cover gilt, oval. 9x12 ins.

499 Another, round form, exquisitely painted with flowers on four-crowned shields, a raised pattern of a floral character between the shields; gilt, altogether superb. Diameter, 12 ins.

500 Fruit-basket on stand, decorated with flowers in colors, the meshes gilt. Height, 6 diameter, 9 ins.

501 Another, similar; same size.

502 One without stand; two handles.

403 Plate ornamented with arabesque border and floral decorations in dead gold, the pattern raised. Diameter, 9 ins.

504 Pair Marcolini plates, painted with bouquet of flowers on the bottom, and smaller flowers on rim; gold edge. Diameter, 9½ ins.   2 p

505 Similar pair.   2 p

506 Similar pair.   2 p

507 Single plate of the king's period; similar decoration, raised rim; same size.

508 Cruet: "Oel" (oil) pencilled on the front, decorated with flowers in colors; handle and lip gilt; high pattern.

509 —— Companion: "Essig" (vinegar) pencilled on the front; similar decoration.

510 Marcolini tea-pot, high ovoid form, painted with a border of flowers in colors; handle and spout ornamented with gold, and gold band top and bottom. Height, 8 ins.

3

511 Bowl of the same period ; a band delicately painted
     with flowers in pale colors, and rim of purple around
     the top, are the decorations. Diameter, 7 ins.

512 Small tea-caddy, similarly decorated.

513 Tea-cup and saucer ; old Meissen ; a lovely moss-rose and
     buds painted on each.

514 Same (old Meissen), with large ornate " H " on each.

514*Same, with three sprigs of flowers (2 of each).   2 p

515 Same, with broad gold band ; on each a yellow rose and
     other flowers. (Cup and saucer).

516 Milk-pitcher with similar decorations ; high pattern.

517 Sugar-bowl, high ovoid form, same decoration.

[The last three lots of old Meissen are extremely fine.]

518 Coffee cups and saucers ; Marcolini ; one cup slightly
     cracked ; painted with simple band of flowers in purple.
     6 of each.   6 p

519 Pair of same, with yellow line on tops ; flowers in colors.
     2 p

520 A handsome cabinet cup and saucer, with a coat-of-arms
     painted on the front of the cup ; broad gold bands on
     both.

521 Blue and white sauce-boat of the king's period ; two
     handles on the sides of the dish ; 9 inches long and 5
     wide (inside the handles). Rare.

522 Bowl with blue border and outside decoration of land-
     scape subject. Diameter, 7 ins.

523 Marcolini Bowl, cobalt blue glaze, with two shield-
     shaped compartments in white, decorated with flower-
     basket. Diameter, 5 ins.

524 Tea-cup, high pattern, blue decorations, with one of
     different form ; ornate letter " K " in front. Very fine.
     2 p

525 Marcolini tea-cups and saucers, not *perfectly* matched,
     but fine (3 of each).   3 p

526 Covered bowl, slightly escalloped top, border of blue in
     ·compartments on cover and dish. Diameter, 7½ ins.

527 Butter-boat on stand, low pattern, handsomely deco-
     rated ; cover mended. Length, 9 ins.

528 TEA-POT, high ovoid pattern, painted with roses and lilies in cobalt blue. Height, 11 ins.

529 HOT-WATER pitcher, with cover; high form, fluted pattern, flowers delicately painted on the pure white ground. Height, 10 ins.

BERLIN PORCELAIN.

530 PUNCH-BOWL, white, with border of basket-work painted green and edged with gold. Diameter, 11½ ins.

531 SOUP TUREEN, raised pattern of vertical lines, with compartments on two sides painted with flowers in colors; handles terminating in flower work applied, with lemon on cover. Very fine. Diameter, 12 ins.

532 Another, pure white, with waved vertical lines in relief; child with flowers on cover. It is also ornamented with a border of basket-work on the body and cover. Diameter, 9 ins.

533 COVERED two-handled bowl of white porcelain. Diameter, 10 ins.

534 PAIR of flower-baskets on stands formed of flags, with Cupids sporting; wreath of flowers painted in colors applied. Extremely fine. Wegeley's mark. Height, 12 ins. 2 p

535 VASE, high ovoid form, fluted pattern, tipped with gold, and enameled in pale green, open cover. Height, 8 ins.

536 TEA-POT, high pattern, painted with exotic birds and butterflies, border of green with gold edges. Height, 6 inches.

537 MILK-PITCHER, metal handle, painted with flowers in colors. Height, 5 inches.

538 CABINET cup and saucer, beautifully decorated in gold and blue; flowers and fruit painted in natural colors, on gold ground; gold lining; handle mended.

539 COFFEE-CUP and saucer; chocolate border, punctuated by small medallions; gold edges.

540 One with similar decorations, a yellow pattern running through the border.

541 Another, with a border divided in sections of orange and blue.

542 PAIR of coffee-cups and saucers, monochrome; flower subject in purple.   2 p

543 TEA-CUP and saucer, with the letter T and wreath of of flowers in green and gold, gold edges.

544 COFFEE-CUP and saucer, with " R " in the same style.

545 One with ornate letter " O " and flowers.

546 TEA-CUPS and saucers; monochrome, painted with flowers in purple, one saucer chipped. (4 of each).   4 p

547 COFFEE-CUP and saucer, painted with border of wild flowers in colors, gold edges.

548 One (monochrome), flowers in purple.

549 TEA-CUPS and saucers, similar to last. (2 of each).   2 p

550 CUP and saucer, high pattern, covered with a bluish-gray lustrous glaze.

551 SUGAR-BOWL; pure white, decorated with vertical lines and scroll-work. Height, 5 inches.

552 BOWL, painted with purple flowers on white ground. Diameter, 6½ inches.

553 PLATE, similarly decorated, octagon shape. 5x5 inches.

554 PAIR of cake plates, enameled border and centre, leaf pattern in medallions, in purple and black; in the field, butterflies delicately pencilled in their natural colors; *extremely fine.* Diameter, 10 inches.   2 p

555 Another pair; duplicates, one slightly chipped.   2 p

556 PLACQUE; escalloped edge, with gold band, decorated, with slightly raised pattern in the paste, and painted in colors; flower subject. Diameter, 14 inches.

MISCELLANEOUS GERMAN.

557 FRANKENTHALL porcelain plate, with the monogram of Carl Theodore; raised basket-work pattern on the rim; flowers in pale colors painted on the bottom. 9 inches.

558 FURSTENBURG porcelain platter; blue decorations on pure white. 11x15 inches.

559 Similar to last, smaller. 10x13 inches.

560 ANDREASBURG porcelain bowl, painted with flowers in purple. Diameter, 8 inches.

561 ANSPACH ? Platter of jasper-ware, blue clay color, decorated with raised ornaments of beads and leaves. 9x13 inches.

562 COFFEE-CUP and saucer, AUS. LIEBE inscribed on the cup; exquisitely painted in India red ; (monochrome); porcelain.

563 MILK jug, with cover ; white porcelain with light blue decorations. Height, 6 inches.

564 BLUE porcelain (with and without marks); two plates (one lozenge shape); soap dish and saltcellar.   4 p

565 BOQUETIERE; quaint old piece of pottery ; Marcolini stand for flower vase.   2 p

VIENNA.

566 COFFEE-CUP and saucer; green glaze, gold edges and centre inscription (Souvenir de Carlsbad)

567 TEA-CUP and saucer (the cup with the Dresden mark) painted with flowers in colors.

568 SAUCERS ; one, celadon glaze, gold decorations.   2 p

569 PLACQUE; blue flowers and border. Diameter, 15 inches.

SPANISH.

570 PLATEAU, deep form, old Saracen pottery, not glazed on the back ; large green flowers rudely drawn ; coat-of-arms on bottom ; date, 1704. Diameter, 12 inches.

571 Similar ; green tulips on rim and bottom. Same size.

572 One with pineapple and shield decorations in green. Same size.

573 LARGE shallow bowl, old Spanish pottery, rudely painted with blue, yellow and green colors ; on the bottom, a woman with harp, trees, etc. 13 inches.

574 PLATEAU or Plaque ; early Spanish ; polychrome ; very rude decorations ; back glazed. Diameter, 14 inches.

ITALIAN POTTERY.

575 PLATE, old Fayence; rim striped with brown and scal
loped, the decorations drawn with a free hand and
well colored; subject of flowers. Diameter, 9 inches.

576 PLATEAU, high rim, escalloped and grooved ; flowers and
castle in yellow and blue, on drab ground. Diameter,
12 inches.

577 OLD Naples vase, high ovoid form with short neck,
griffin-head handles rising to the top, decorated in the
paste with borders and festoons of flowers, afterwards
painted and gilt, the bottom mended; extremely fine.
Height, 10 inches.

578 MAJOLICA Pitcher, antique pattern. The body is oviform, on a small base ; the mouth is large, with a long
spreading lip ; below the handle is a mask of Medusa,
the decorations in low-relief, as well as color, are
borrowed from the antique, the subject of the former
being drawn from their mythology. The general color
is cream-yellow, the painted portions blue-yellow and
black. A real gem. Height, 16 inches.

579 FAIENCE plates, open borders, decorated with roses in
relief; on the bottom, flowers in purple and green,
prettily painted. Diameter, 9 inches.   2 p

580 PLATEAU (Plaque), high vertical rim, dark glaze; beautiful agate centre, unknown fabrique. Diameter, 14 in.

581 MAJOLICA vase, with cover, decorations in bas-relief;
fine agate glaze.

582 —— Melon, on plate.

583 —— One without plate, smaller.

584 PORCELAIN Pineapple.

585 —— Bird.

586 —— Fish. Length, 13 inches.

587 —— One. Length, 12 inches.

588 —— One. Length, 9 inches.

FRENCH.

589 GOLD and salmon plain porcelain covered vase on tripod support; handles, two cherub heads. Height, 8 in.

590 —·— Companion; faulty.

591 COFFEE-cup and saucer, gold and blue porcelain, Egyptian design (Sphinx head); very beautiful and rare, but wants the handle.

592 Another coffee-cup and saucer, gold and blue, with a zone of flowers in their natural colors painted on each. A beautiful transparent porcelain.

593 TRIPOD cup, with saucer to match; dolphin handle of solid brass, gilt, in place of the original; landscape, with large bird in the foreground; all in natural colors. Fine porcelain.

594 Another, smaller porcelain cup and saucer, the border in gold and colors, with a medallion picture in black, transferred.

595 PORCELAIN flower-holder or boquetiere, with 5 mouths painted in colors and gilt; the body represents tufts of green flags on salmon-colored base. Signed J. P. (J. Petit Belleville). Rare.

596 PAIR of gilt porcelain 2-handle vases; the body has a green celadon glaze, on which is painted on one side the panoply of Cupid, and on the other a figure subject, gilt. Height, 12 inches.   2 p

OLD MOUSTIERS.

597 PLATEAU, high escalloped rim, with painting of flowers and scrolls. On the bottom grotesque figures—men, animals, and birds in monocrome (orange); pottery. Diameter, 12 inches.

598 PLATE, same fabrique and style of decoration. Diameter, 10 inches.

599 PAIR of plates of this rare pottery, polychrome—orange, green, and blue on pale pink ground; grotesque subjects as before, etc. Diameter, 10½ inches.   2 p

600 One similar; bright colors on drab ground. Same size.

ROUEN, VINCENNES, AND OTHER FACTORIES.

602 PLATEAU, wide rim, the edge raised and scalloped; a sun-flower and arabesque painted in orange color on the bottom. *Carmelite* pottery, Rouen. Diameter, 16 in.

603 PLATES, scalloped rim, decorated with flowers; below the rim a scroll border in blue; within a circle on the bottom, a landscape in bright colors, slightly raised; polychrome. *Vincennes.* Diameter, 9 inches.   2 p

604 PAIR of Biscuit figures, painted and glazed; young man with wallet and staff; young woman with flax and spindle. Height, 15 inches.   2 p

605 HEREND (Hungary) porcelain cups and saucers, three of each. The form is octagon, a different decoration on each of the 8 sides; a beautiful border on the inside of the cups and outside of the saucers. The colors are enamels, and the work *extremely fine.*   3 p

606 CUP and saucer like last; handle of the cup wanting.

607 GROUPE. Porcelain, cobbler and bird, *Ludwigsburg.* A fine piece. Height, 10 inches.

ENGLISH.

608 WEDGWOOD. Milk pitcher, high ovoid pattern, divided handle; cover with seated female; black basalt. Height, 8 inches.

609 —— Another, without cover, low pattern; figures in low-relief; black basalt. 4 inches.

610 —— One high ovoid without cover, fluted pattern; black basalt. Height, 6 inches.

611 —— Similar milk pitcher, the handle decorated with leaves; black basalt. Height, 5 inches.

612 —— Same as last.

613 —— Tea-pot; seated female on cover; black basalt. Height, 4½ inches.

614 —— Another, with small fluted lines radiated; on the cover, which has a slight crack, a lion lying down; black basalt. Height, 6 inches.

615 WEDGWOOD. Creamer, low pattern, plain ; black basalt.

616 —— Small pitcher with wide open top; black basalt. Height, 4 inches.

617 —— Pitcher with narrow top, high pattern, the handle springing from a lion's mask; partly enclosed lip ; black basalt. Height, 8 inches.

618 —— Tea-kettle ; copper bail willow wound ; on cover, a seated female ; running around the body, bas-relief decoration of garlands of flowers hanging in festoons, and circles both beaded and plain; black basalt. Extremely fine and valuable.

619 —— Open vase on square stand, signed WEDGWOOD & BENTLEY ETRVRIA. It is in the Antique style, with a flat band around its greatest diameter decorated with bas-relief festoons of drapery, not uncommon on Cinerary Urns; black basalt. Height, 5 inches.

[This is extremely rare and valuable.]

620 WELLINGTON sugar-bowl with oval medallion, representing the bust of Wellington between Britannia and Fame on one side, with inscription within similar oval on the other. Lion heads as handles on the bowl, a bouquet of flowers serving the same purpose on the cover ; laurels and other floral decorations in profusion covering all ; black basalt. Diameter, 6 inches.

621 WEDGEWOOD SUGAR-bowl of black basalt with bas-relief figure ; subjects in panels on two sides, boys playing with a lion, etc. Same size as last.

622 —— Tea-pot ; yellow jasper, with belt of pale green grapes on the vine, in high-relief; quaint decorations on the spout and cover handle; it has a slight crack near the handle. Rare.

623 —— Tureen (3 pieces). White pottery with brown decorations of landscape subjects and festoons of vines ; faulty.

624 —— Tea-pot ; blue and white, with Bacchic subjects on the body ; the Welsh plumes and crosses on the cover ; all in relief. Very fine and rare.

625 LOWESTOFT Tea-pot; white porcelain with roses on the sides and a narrow circle of floral decorations on the top, which is repeated on the cover; twisted handles with raised and painted decorations at the 4 terminations. Height, 6 inches.

626 —— Tea-cup, blue and gold porcelain.

627 SMALL pitcher; English bisque; bas-relief of Cupids at play, etc.; a circle of acanthus leaves and vines at bottom and top. Very fine. Height, 4 inches.

628 WATER-Pitcher; blue and gold lustre, with rose-buds and fruit in bas-relief, natural colors. *Extremely fine.* Height, 7 inches.

629 OLD Staffordshire dinner-plate; pottery; variegated colors, in Majolica style.

630 —— Punch bowl, blue and white; pottery. Diameter, 9½ inches.

631 —— Platter, blue decorations, landscape subject, reticulated border; the lower circle of meshes closed; pottery. Length, 10 inches.

633 OLD WORCESTER Fruit-basket and stand; porcelain; an elaborate pattern delicately pencilled in gold on salmon-colored bands; open border. Diameter, 10 inches.

634 —— Companion basket; broken.

635 —— Similar fruit-basket and stand, but smaller, and oval in form; one handle gone. 7x10 inches.

636 —— Pair of oval baskets and stands; salmon and gold porcelain. 6x9 inches.

637 —— Another pair, same in all respects; the handle of one basket wanting.

638 —— Pair of pickle-dishes, shell-shaped, same ware.

639 —— Large soup-tureen; cover and stand; same ware. Diameter of bowl, 11 inches; of stand, 13 inches.

640 —— Covered vase, salmon and gold porcelain, dolphins' heads for handles. Height, 1 foot; diameter, 9 inches.

641 —— Another, exactly similar.

642 —— Coffee-cups and saucers (salmon and gold), 6 of each. 6 p

643 —— Others, imperfect. (7 of each). 7 p

644 Old Worcester Tea-cups and saucers (6 of each) of this
rare and beautiful porcelain.   6 p
645 —— Others, same in all respects (3 of each).   3 p
646 —— The same, slightly cracked.   3 p
647 —— Saucers, salmon and gold.   10 p
648 —— Plates, same ware; small deep pattern.   6 p
649 —— Same repeated.   6 p
650 —— Repetition of last.   6 p
651 —— Same.   6 p
652 —— Same.   4 p

653 Faience; plates with the mark of Robert Hollish; yellow ground, with flowers painted within shield and
circular-shaped borders in bright colors on white; scalloped rims. Diameter, 9 inches.   2 p

654 Tureen; cream-colored pottery, with twisted handles,
pineapple on cover. Very light fabrique; believed to
be a piece of Josiah Wedgwood's "Queen's Ware."
Length, outside of handles, 12 inches.

655 Placque; white porcelain, decorated with a vine running
around the rim between a broad and narrow band; all
green. Very fine. Diameter, 17 inches.

SELECTION OF OBJECTS OF VARIED CHARACTER.

656 Fine Bust of Eugene De La Croix (eminent artist); about half the natural size. Modeled by *T. Pollet;* executed by Calla, Paris, 1840 ; in Berlin iron bronzed.

657 Fine Book-rack, in black walnut, richly carved.

658 Chinese Lantern. Very fine.

659 Solid silver gold-lined sugar-basket.

660 Set of chess-men of medium size ; good examples of Chinese carving in ivory. 32 pieces. By the set.

661 Repetition of last.

662 Pair elegant Japanese porcelain vases; beautifully enameled with large insects and flowers; the handles consist of elephant heads, with rings pendant from the trunk. Height, 14 inches.   2 p

663 Pair fine Chinese porcelain cuspidors, oviform body, with spreading base and top ; superbly enameled with oriental scenes in panels. Height, 14 inches.   2 p

664 Repetition of last.   2 p

665 Chinese Fan ; carved ivory stick and painted feathers. *Extra fine.*

666 Embroidered Fan ; carved ivory stick and white satin.

667 One similar, with spangles.

668 French carved ivory fan. Fine and valuable.

669 Sandalwood Fan ; every part handsomely carved ; Chinese. Valuable.

670 Painted Oriental fans ; all with ivory sticks.   4 p

CLOISONNE ENAMELS.

[The enameled bronzes of China are indisputably superior to any other. This is especially true of work done in the peculiar manner called cloisonne, in which the different colors are enclosed within

their proper bounds by a net-work of wires, which form the pattern. How expensive such works must be, will be understood
when we remember that designs in different colors can only be
completed by repeated baptisms of fire, in which more are destroyed
than successfully made. The beautiful examples that follow are
of the very finest quality at present produced. To say that they
are fully equal to the ancient enamels, would be to say too much.
Yet it would be difficult to point out the quality in which they are
inferior. Certainly not in gracefulness of form, or in elegance of
design, or in correct drawing. In thoroughness of workmanship
they are not deficient, and hardly in the single quality of color.
Modern work undoubtedly lacks the tone of the old ; yet who can
say how much of this is not the work of time ? These enamels are
on bronze, with gilt bottoms and tops, the gilding extending a con-
siderable way down the necks into the interior of the vases. They
. are from Pekin and all of Chinese manufacture.]

671 PAIR card receivers ; enameled with fowls and foliage on
turquoise ground ; a pattern of flowers and vines on black
ground on the inside, and different decorations on the
outside of the rim. Diameter, about 6 inches. 2 p

672 A pair of similar receivers ; decorated with a bird standing composedly on a rock under a pine tree, regarding
a disappointed prowler. 2 p

673 PAIR of two-handled vases, oval in form, a burnished
band at the base of the neck, which expands moderately
to its vertical rim, with Greek border ; the decorations
in ultra-marine and other bright colors on turquoise
ground. Height, 9½ inches. 2 p

674 A pair of the same form and size ; the decorations in
sections on shields and medallions. 2 p

675 PAIR of oviform vases, without handles, with slightly
spreading tops, different shades of blue with green and
red running through the pattern. Height, 8½ in. 2 p

676 A pair of the same form and size ; decorated with flowering shrubs in their natural colors on pale ash-colored
ground, the cloisons forming a labyrinthine pattern.
Very beautiful. 2 p

677 A PAIR of vases, oval to the base, with long narrow necks,
the decorations closely resembling those last described.
Height, 9 inches. 2 p

678 Another pair in same form and colors, but with different decorations; large and highly-colored ducks being conspicuous objects. Same size. 2 p

679 A similar pair, with fishes, etc. 2 p

680 Pair of magnificent vases, of cylindrical form, slightly contracting at the base, the neck spreading at the top, with vertical rim; exotic flowers and colored borders forming the subject of the decorations, the prevailing color being a fine turquoise blue. Height, 14 in. 2 p

681 A pair of very beautiful vases, of high ovoid form, with long necks of even width to the top; the body of the vase is adorned with representations of oriental works in jade, cloisonne enamels, and wood-lacquers, in proper colors on *light* ground; the borders and neck being in bright colors on *black* ground. Extremely fine and valuable. Height, 13 inches. 2 p

682 Pair of vases of slightly ovoid shape, with short, thick necks and spreading, scalloped tops; decorated with flowering shrubs in vertical sections on ultra-marine; turquoise and vermilion ground. Height, 7½ in. 2 p

683 Another pair, similar, with the same decorations on different ground. 2 p

684 Pair of vases of oviform shape, with narrow necks; slightly spreading tops, with floral and arabesque decorations on vermilion ground; the only pair of this color in the collection. Height, 8 inches. 2 p

685 Pair of similar vases, with ash-colored ground. Same size. 2 p

686 Pair of the same size and form, with a circle at the base of the neck, worked in a mosaic pattern; the ground a deep turquoise blue, with decorations in the form of medallions and birds on the wing. 2 p

687 Pair of extremely fine vases of globular (slightly ovoid) form, the neck in two sections and long; superbly enameled in every part, with floral, arabesque, and oriental decorations in bright colors on deep turquoise ground. Height, 12 inches. 2 p

688 A Pair of the same shape and size, with only a slight difference in the decorations. 2 p

689 Pair of fine bottle-shaped vases, with exquisite decorations of a floral character on ash-colored ground; 2 borders and circle of oriental characters on the neck. Height, 9 inches. 2 p

690 Pair of oviform vases, rather broad in contour; short, thick neck spreading at the top with burnished rim, enameled with fishes and crabs in bright colors on blue ground. Height, 9½ inches. 2 p

691 Pair of very elegant two-handle vases, high ovoid pattern, beautifully decorated with arabesque and other figures on shields and medallions. 7 inches. 2 p

692 Another pair, same in every respect. 2 p

693 Tea-Pot, low pattern, divided handle, gilt; enameled spout and cover; the body superbly enameled with light medallions and borders on deep ultra-marine blue ground. Height to top of bail, 7 inches.

694 Another tea-pot like last.

695 Pair of magnificent vases, divided vertically by four deep gores into six lobes extending from base to top, the neck broad and marked at the base by a circle of vermilion-red; the body decorated with exotic birds and flowers in their natural colors on light blue ground. Height, 16 inches. 2 p

696 Pair of broad oviform vases on narrow base; short, thick neck, the rim at bottom and top broad and decorated with Greek border, incised; the surface enameled with birds and flowers in bright colors on turquoise ground. Height, 12 inches. 2 p'

697 Similar pair, the borders enameled. 2 p

698 Fine pair of vases of the same general description as last, but smaller. Height, 9 inches. 2 p

699 Superb pair vases, cylindrical in form and beautifully enameled; the decorations consist of butterflies, flowers and berries, drawn and colored with great fidelity to nature. The general color is a deep turquoise blue. Height, 15 inches. 2 p

700 Pair of beautiful, long-necked vases of a light ash-color; the body decorated with trees and flowers; the necks with borders and circles of a varied character. Height, 9 inches. 2 p
701 Pair of two-handle vases, blue enamel, with shields and medallions of fanciful patterns. Height, 8 inches. 2 p
702 Similar pair, with decorations of a floral character. 2 p

---

FAIENCES.

LAURENS.

[Faiencés D'Art Bourg-la-Reine ; Seine.]

703 Pair fine two-handle vases, enameled with flowers and butterflies in their proper colors on variegated blue-tinted ground. Height, 19 ins. 2 p
704 Pair extremely fine vases of cylindrical form, with wide tops and slightly contracting base ; green enamel ground decorated with birds and flowering vines. Height, 17 ins. 2 p
705 Pair buff flower-pots, painted with birds and flowers, tortoise-shell glaze on inside and outside. Diameter and height, 8 ins. 2 p

THEODORE DECK, PARIS.

706 Pair vases, high ovoid pattern, with masks holding rings, attached in the nature of handles, decorated with a quaint pattern of arabesques and flowers, with large medallions in lighter colors on the sides. Height, 12 ins. 2 p
707 Another pair, ovoid form, broad in cantour, light buff ground with raised enamel flowers and birds in natural colors. Height, 14 ins. 2 p
708 Single vase of this beautiful Faiencé, with borders and belts of the most exquisite enameling on pale buff, form like last. Same height.
709 Bon-boniere, square form butterfly on cover. 6½x6½ ins.
710 Another, round, smaller.

GALLÈ A NANCY.

711 BLUE pitcher, with cover; twisted handle. Height, 13 ins.

712 GREEN pitcher, also with cover, enameled with masks and scrolls in relief and colors. Same height.

713 PLAQUE painted with three sprigs of flowers on light ground, open rim. Diameter, about 15 ins.

714 Another, same decorations and size.

715 ANTIQUE ewer, blue decorations. Extra fine.

716 WATER-CARRIER, with twisted handle over the top, cover, and spout; also blue. Extra fine.

717 COVERED jar, with a belt of open work near the top, cover with detached relief work, lion, etc., green enamel glaze. Extra fine.

718 OBLONG basket, rose color.

719 PAIR tall candlesticks, painted with blue.

720 PAIR figures, holding coupes; blue and green decorations. Beautiful.   2 p

721 CAT; zebra.

---

722 PALLISSY vase, cylindrical form, contracting at base and top, covered with shells, lizards, etc., applied to the surface, and painted in the colors of nature. Remarkable and rare. Height, 20 ins.

723 PAIR of magnificent vases of ovoid form, broad at the bottom, enameled with leaf patterns and artistic designs in the form of mosaic or cloisonne work, producing a charming effect; ground ultra-marine blue. Height, 12 ins.   2 p

---

JAPANESE WOOD LACQUERS.

723* HANDSOME picnic-box, mother-of-pearl and ivory inlay on black lacquer; silver-mounted, with lock and key— with contents, viz., six decorated cherry-wood plates, bon–bon box, saki bowl, long boxes, clylindrical and square, and cigar-case.

724 Similar in all respects.

725 Similar in all respects.

726 Similar in all respects.

727 Similar in all respects.

728 Similar in all respects.

729 SHAWL-BOX, with gold and colored lacquer ornaments on black ground; inside, aventurine lacquer, decorated; silver-mounted, with lock and key. 11x16 ins. Very fine.

730 Another box, similar. 9x15 ins.

731 Another, similar. 7x13 ins.

732 REVOLVING-TOP centre-table of rich brown lacquer, decorated with embossed ornaments on black ground. Diameter, 27 ins.

733 Similar to last.

734 Similar to last.

735 NEST of handsome square trays with rounded corners, in black lacquer richly decorated with birds and flowers in gold and colors. 18x18 ins.   2 p

736 NEST, similar to last.   2 p

737 NEST, similar.   2 p

738 NEST, similar.   2 p

739 NEST, similar.   2 p

740 SMALL cabinet, black and gold lacquer, on stand, silver-mounted, with folding doors; box on top with lifting cover.

741 Similar cabinet, aventurine lacquer.

742 Same as last.

743 SMALL silver-mounted gold and black lacquer cabinet, crests on all sides, the drawers decorated with gold butterflies on aventurine ground ; handle on top. 6x7 ins.

744 Same in all respects.

745 Similar, differently decorated.

746 Same as last.

747 PAIR of same.   2 p

748 Another pair.   2 p

749 PORTABLE cabinet, sliding front, three drawers behind, black lacquer, with decorations in gold and colors. 5x7 ins.

750 Repetition of last.

751 Another, same in all respects.

752 PAIR, similar.   2 p

753 GOLD and black lacquer silver-mounted box, with aventurine lacquer lining ; containing tray and two jewel boxes. Very handsome. 6x9 ins.

754 Repetition of last.

755 Same, but differently decorated, on this a frog embossed in gold and colors. Very fine.

756 Pair of same.   2 p

757 GOLD and black lacquer box with lock and key ; within, two decorated lacquer boxes with sliding covers ; subject of exterior decoration landscapes with birds, embossed in gold and vermilion. Very fine. 6x8 ins.

758 Repetition of last.

759 PAIR of similar boxes, differently ornamented. Equally fine.   2 p

760 Another pair.   2 p

761 PAIR black lacquer paper and letter-boxes, with inlaid and painted ornaments. 9x10 ins.   2 p

762 Repetition of same.   2 p

763 Others, differently decorated.   2 p

764 Same, with shells, inlaid.   2 p

765 CIGAR-BOX, gold and black lacquer, with ivory and mother-of-pearl ornaments inlaid; lock and key. 9x11 ins.

766 Repetition of last.

767 Same.

768 Another.

769 NEST of gold and black lacquer trays. 10x10 ins.   2 p

770 Same.   2 p

771 Same.   2 p

772 Same, with two nests of brown lacquer boxes.   10 p

773 Same.   10 p

774 Same.   10 p

775 HANDSOME circular tray, with boxes (4) forming a circle, gold and black lacquer.   5 p

776 Similar tray, containing four fine lacquer boxes.   5 p

777 NEST of oval black and gold lacquer trays, largest 15 inches diameter, containing 1 vermilion lacquer saki bowl, nest of three scalloped bowls, nest of 3 round boxes, with covers, and 1 telescopic box 6 ins. long. All handsomely decorated.   10 p

778 Same.

779 Same.

780 Same.   10 p

781 Same.   10 p

782 Same.   10 p

783 Same.   10 p

784 Same.   10 p

785 Same.   10 p

786 Same.   10 p

787 Same.   10 p

788 Same.   10 p

789 NEST of oblong vermilion lacquer Trays, largest, 15 inches diameter, containing 6 best quality vermilion-lacquer tea-cups and saucers.   14 p

[NOTE.—No fear need be entertained of putting scalding water into vessels of this lacquer, which is especially made and adapted for the purpose.]

790 Same as 789.   14 p

791 Same.   14 p

792 Same.   14 p

793 Same.   14 p

794 Same.   14 p

TEXTILE AND OTHER FABRICS.

FROM AFRICA AND THE ORIENT.

795 Rich white cashmere, embroidered Burnous cloak, Turkish manufacture.

796 Embroidered Burnous cloak ; Tunis fabric, trimmed with hand work.

797 One of white Camel's hair, also from Tunis.

798 Another, same fabric ; all silk.

799 Small Burnous Cloak, same fabric.

800 Others, same as last.

801 Pair of Turkish Embroidered Pine-apple Handkerchiefs.
2 p

802 Pair of Embroidered Neck-ties.   Turkish.   2 p

803 Another pair, same.   2 p

804 Others, same.   4 p

805 Large Japanese Sash, black satin, embroidered.

806 Pair Canton Crape Scarfs, embroidered.   2 p

807 Another pair, same.   2 p

808 Others, same.   2 p

809 Pair, same; smaller size.   2 p

810 Others, same.   5 p

811 Half-dozen Japanese Colored Silk Handkerchiefs.   6 p

812 Repetition of last.   6 p

813 Same.   6 p

814 Same.   6 p

815 Same.   6 p

816 Others, same as last.   12 p

817 Another lot, same.   11 p

818 Gentleman's Smoking Cap ; fine red and gold, with tassel.

819 Same, different color.

820 Same.

821 Same.

822 Same.

823 Same.

824 Pair Embroidered Turkish Slippers, not made up.

825 Pair Velvet Shoes, Chinese.

826 Gentlemen's plain Turkish Slippers.   2 prs

827 Others, same.   2 prs

828 Pair of same, embroidered.
829 Others, same as last.   2 prs
830 Ladies' Slippers, embroidered, Turkish.   2 prs
831 Others, same.   3 prs
832 Same, plain.   2 prs
833 Pair of Ladies' Slippers, embroidered, morocco.
834 Chinese Straw Shoes.   2 p
835 Turkish Slippers, silk velvet, embroidered with gold ; boat shape.   2 prs
836 Same, with back ; purple and gold.   2 prs
837 Another pair, same.
838 Pair, same ; red and gold, embroidered.
839 Others, same as last.   2 prs
840 Others (one pair green).   2 prs
841 Half-Slippers, green.   4 prs
842 Slippers, purple and gold, embroidered.   2 prs
843 Same ; blue.   2 prs
844 Same ; red.   2 prs
845 Same ; silver and gold, embroidered.   3 prs
846 Same in all respects.   2 prs
847 Same ; blue, silver and gold.   2 prs
848 Same : purple.   2 prs
849 Pair Red Slippers from Tunis.
850 Slippers ; shop worn.   3 prs

STEREOSCOPIC INSTRUMENTS, VIEWS, ETC.

[The Views are all perfect, and many of them rare.]

851 Rosewood Skeleton Stereoscope.
852 Patent Kaleidescope on stand.
853 Stereoscopic Views, Spain, etc. Glass.   33 p
854 Same ; Alpine Club ; views in Paris, etc.   24 p
855 Same ; Statuary and Mammoth Cave.   32 p
856 Same (Imperial) ; Yo-Semite, etc.   16 p
857 Same ; Yo-semite, etc.   36 p
858 Same ; Lakes, Mountains, etc.   44 p
859 Same ; Flowers, Frost-work, and Actresses.   22 p
860 Same ; colored Groups and Scenery.   24 p
861 Same ; Dresden Groups. (Very fine).   21 p
862 Same ; Transparent.   18 p
863 Same ; Nudes, Pictures, etc.   52 p
864 Same ; Actresses, etc.   26 p

ORIENTAL AND ALGERINE TEXTILES.

865 EMBROIDERED lamp-stand of Turkish manufacture.

866 TURKISH gold and silk embroidered table-cover. (Red.) Small.

867 Same: silk ; blue with red centre.   Small.

868 Same ; silk ; black centre.   do

869 Same ; drab felt embroidered in colors.   Small.

870 Same ; similar style, medium size.

871 CHAIR cover ; with back and seat.   Embroidered ; Turkish.

872 PAIR, gold embroidered red silk velvet sofa-cushions ; Turkish.   2 p

873 PAIR of same ; purple.   2 p

874 SOFA-CUSHION ; leather, with embroidery in silver. Turkish.

875 TRAVELING-BAG ; embroidered with silk.   Turkish.

876 EMBROIDERED looking-glass case, velvet.   Turkish.

877 SMOKING-Cap ; embroidered.   Chinese.

878 Same.

879 Same, with tassels.   Turkish.

880 Others, similar.   4 p

881 LADIES' velvet caps, embroidered with gold.   2 p

882 CUSHION ; blue satin embroidered with gold.

883 CHINESE silk screens (not mounted).   3 p

884 INDIAN bead table-covers (large and small).   2 p

885 TURKISH embroidered felt table-cover ; drab worked in colors ; large size.

886 ALGERINE curtains ; gold and black stripes.   5 p

887 Same ; blue and white, white, and white and black.   3 p

888 ALGERINE Opera-cloaks (Burnous), white and silver stripes.

889 Repetition of last.

890 Same, with gold stripes.

891 Repetition of last.

892 ALGERINE Opera-cloaks (small stripes), white and black.

893 Same. 2 p

894 ANOTHER, gold and black, large stripes.

895 PAIR of same. 2 p

896 PAIR of same ; blue and silver ; small. 2 p

897 BURNOUS cloak ; white ; hand-trimmed. Tunis.

898 Same.

899 Repetition of last.

900 Same ; red and white.

901 PAIR of same. (Red and white). 2 p

902 ONE of the same ; heavy, of the finest materials ; red and white striped, trimmed with gold.

903 ONE heavy white Burnous opera-cloak trimmed with blue.

904 CASHMERE colored opera-cloak. Tunis.

905 OTHERS, faded, a lot of. 5 p

906 PERSIAN scarf shawl.

907 PAIR of same. 2 p

908 Same ; small breakfast shawls. 2 p

909 Another pair. 2 p

910 CAMEL'S hair scarf. Embroidered by hand.

911 Another ; Persian.

912 Repetition of last.

913 CHINESE sable. 2 p

WOOD LACQUERS OF JAPAN.

914 NEST of oblong black-lacquer trays, containing 6 plum-tree wood-covered cups and saucers ornamented with gold lacquer. (Counting 20 pieces) sold as 8 p

915 Same. 8 p

916 Same. 8 p

917 Same. 8 p

918 Same. 8 p

919 NEST of 3 ; best quality ; vermilion-lacquer saki-cups ; lining of gold lacquer, embossed with exquisite decorative figures. 3 p

920 NEST of 3 similar cups, with different decorations. 3 p

921 SQUARE box of gold and black lacquer, lined with aventurine; cover handsomely decorated with landscape subject. Diameter, 9½ inches.

922 NEST of small oval red lacquer-trays, and contents. 12 plum-wood plates with gilded lacquer ornaments, and nest of 3 black and gold lacquer boxes.   17 p

923 Similar nest, trays of black and gold lacquer.   17 p

924 Same as last.   17 p

925 NEST of vermilion lacquer trays (15 in) and contents. 6 covered vermilion bowls.   8 p

926 Repetition of last.   18 p

927 Same.   8 p

928 Same, black lacquer with gold decorations; contents, twelve pieces plum-tree wood plates and cups.   14 p

929 Repetition.   14 p

930 Same.   14 p

931 Same.   14 p

932 Same.   14 p

933 Same.   14 p

934 GOLD and brown lacquer bowls, in nests.   3 p

935 Repetition of last.   3 p

936 Same.   3 p

937 Same.   3 p

938 Same.   3 p

939 Same.   3 p

940 Same.   3 p

941 Same.   3 p

942 Same.   3 p

943 Same.   3 p

944 Same.   3 p

945 Same.   3 p

946 Similar bowls, scalloped, also in nests.   3 p

947 Same.   3 p

948 Same.   3 p

949 Same.   3 p

950 Same.   3 p

951 Same.   3 p

952 NEST of fine vermilion lacquer bowls decorated inside with figures in gold.   3 p

953 Same.   3 p

954 SAKI-CUPS, in fine vermilion lacquer, inside decoration of
    various figures in gold.   5 p
955 Same.   5 p
956 Same.   5 p
957 Same.   5 p
958 Same.   5 p
959 Same.   5 p
960 Same.   5 p
961 Same.   5 p
962 Same.   5 p
963 Same.   5 p
964 Same.   5 p
965 Same.   5 p
966 Same.   5 p
967 Same.   5 p
968 Same.   5 p
969 Same.   5 p
970 Same   5 p
971 Same.   5 p
972 Same.   5 p
973 NEST of oval black and gold lacquer trays. Diameter,
    14 ins., and contents, viz., nest of boxes, nest of scal-
    loped bowls, and telescopic box.   8 p
974 Same.   8 p
975 Same.   8 p
976 Same.   8 p
977 Same.   8 p
978 NEST of similar trays, and contents, viz., nest of three
    round boxes, telescopic box, cigar-case, all in black and
    gold lacquer, and plum-tree wood cup and saucer. 9 p
979 Same.   9 p
980 Same.   9 p
981 NEST of similar trays and contents, viz., nest of three
    scalloped bowls, nest of three round boxes, cigar-case,
    telescopic box, and puff-powder box, all in gold and
    black lacquer.   11 p
982 Same.   11 p
983 Same.   11 p
984 Same.   11 p

985 Nest of similar trays, and contents, viz., diced pattern black and silver tea-caddy, telescopic box, cigar-case, and three round-cornered boxes of different sizes. 8 p

986 Oval tray, similar, and contents, viz., nest of six vermilion-lined bowls, the largest having a cover, round flat box, diced pattern, black and silver tea-caddy and cigar-case. 10 p

987 Cigar-box, black and gold lacquer, pierced for four and a half dozen cigars, with lock and key; inlaid with ivory and mother-of-pearl. 8x11 ins.

988 Similar to last.

989 Pair black and gold lacquer card-boxes, with lifting cover, silver-mounted, lock and key; containing boxes for two packs. 2 p

990 Pair, same as last. 2 p

991 Pair of silver-mounted, gold and black lacquer miniature cabinets, with lock and key, containing three drawers. 6x7 ins. 2 p

992 Pair of black and gold lacquer boxes, with lifting cover, silver-mounted, with lock and key, containing two decorated boxes with sliding covers. 2 p

993 Pair, same as last.

994 Fine black lacquer papetiere, containing paper-weight or follower in black lacquer, the cover inlaid and decorated with exquisite taste.

995 Same.
996 Same.
997 Same.
998 Same.
999 Same.
1000 Same.

1001 Nest of fine quality black and gold lacquer trays, with embossed decorations inside. Diameter, 11 inches. 2 p

1002 Repetition of last. 2 p

1003 Nest of rich brown and gold lacquer, oblong trays, decorated inside with landscape subjects in embossed gold. Diameter, 17½ inches. 2 p

1004 Repetition of last. 2 p
1005 Similar nest, in black and gold lacquer. 2 p
1006 Same as last. 2 p
1007 Same. 2 p

1008 Nest of similar oblong black and gold lacquer trays, ornamented inside. Diameter, 15 inches. 2 p

1009 Same as last. 2 p

1010 Same. 2 p

1011 Nest of gold and black lacquer oval trays, decorated inside. Diameter, 15 inches. 2 p

1012 Same. 2 p

1013 Same. 2 p

1014 Same. 2 p

1015 Same. 2 p

1016 Same. 2 p

1017 Same. 2 p

1018 Same. 2 p

1019 Same. 2 p

1020 Same. 2 p

1021 Same. 2 p

1022 Same. 2 p

1023 Same. 2 p

1024 Same. 2 p

1025 Same. 2 p

1026 Set of plum-tree wood saucers, ornamented with designs in gold lacquer. 32 p

1027 Set of small spherical boxes in gold and black lacquer, in 24 nests of three boxes each. 24 p

1028 Nests of brown lacquer, vermilion-lined bowls, the external bowl of each nest having a lid with gold-lacquer decorations. 14 p

1029 Same. 24 p

1030 Two and a half dozen cylindrical boxes, of telescopic form, in black and gold lacquer. 6 inches high. 30 p

1031 Same. 24 p

1032 Nests of handsome round boxes in brown and gold lacquer, with gilded knobs, two boxes in a nest, external box 6 inches diameter. 4 p

1033 Same, very slightly smaller. 30 p

1034 Same. 25 p

1035 Twenty-two nests of dark-brown lacquer boxes, decorated with gold, each nest consisting of three boxes, external box 5 inches diameter. 22 p

1036 Saki tub of ceremony, black and gold lacquer, with granulated interior surface, lined with gold. About 4x6 inches.

[Used on wedding occasions.]

1037 Similar.

1038 Similar.

1039 Similar.

1040 Same, but with a section decorated with white and black lacquer in squares.

1041 Same as last.

1042 Bon-bon boxes, circular form, decorated lacquer on cherry wood. 10 p

1043 Repetition of last. 10 p

COINS, MEDALS, JEWELRY, ETC.

1044 Gold Stater of Alexander (Magnus), obv. helmed head rev. winged Victory and ALEXANDER.

[A perfect example, fresh from Asia Minor, as are the two following lots] :

1045 Silver coin (drachma) of the Ephesian Colony of Aradus in Phœnicia; obv. Bee within beaded circle; rev palm-tree, stag, and the name of the colony. Well preserved and rare.

1046 Rare copper coins of Ancient Egypt; the city of Antioch; Erythrea in Ionia; and Persia; one with heads of Antony and Cleopatra; one with a centaur drawing the bow, etc.; remarkable and valuable, deserving the attention of connoisseurs. 12 p

1047 Copies of rare and inaccessible gold and silver coins in the possession of the British Museum. 12 p

1048 A small collection of silver and copper coins and medals, ancient and modern, among them U. S. cents of 1808–9–10–11, etc., of good quality. 40 p

1049 Silver coins (denarii) from the collection of Sir Edmund Temple, sold in New York in 1865; they are in the envelopes used at the sale, and with them is a catalogue where the description of each will be found. The next lot is from the same source, and the same remarks will apply. 20 p

1049* Brass coins referred to above. 19 p

[The two lots to be sold together, making with the catalogue 40 pieces.]

1050 A miscellaneous collection of coins and medals, nearly all from the Stenz sale, in original envelopes. A few American coins in the lot, including a cent of 1793. 228 p

1050* Eighteen karat gold watch in running order; hunting case, a pretty little affair one inch in diameter.

1051 Turkish jewelry box; pearl inlay.

1052 Same; tortoise shell (ground).

1053 Portmonnaies; embroidered with silver. 2 p

1054 Same. 2 p

1055 Same; embroidered with gold. 2 p

1056 Same do 2 p

1057 Same do 2 p

1058 Same; velvet; large size. 2 p

1059 Same as last. 3 p

1060 Ottar of Rose; beautiful cut-glass bottles. 2 p

1061 Same. 2 p

1062 Same. 2 p

1063 Set crystal jewelry, silver-mounted; Chinese; complete with necklace and bracelet.

1064 Crystal jewelry, gold-mounted; Chinese.

1065 Amber jewelry, dark and light; Turkish. 2 p

1066 Silver ear-rings; Turkish. 2 pairs

1067 Shell Bracelets and necklets, gold thread; three of each. 6 p

1068 Coral bracelets and necklets, mounted on gold thread; five of each. 10 p

1069 Sandal-wood card-cases, large and small. 2 p

1070 Ivory carved Chinese card cases. 2 p

1071 Same; with one same Japanese. 2 p

1072 SET pearl card-counters, carved.
1073 PAIR Japanese napkin-rings, pearl inlay. 2 p
1074 CHINESE " nine-stick" puzzle ; ivory on silk cords ; fine.
1075 PAIR ivory inlaid crochet-needles. 2 p
1076 JAPANESE bronze fruit-knife handles. 10 p
1077 Repetition of last. 10 p

WOOD LACQUERS.

1078 SILVER-MOUNTED work-box in gold and black lacquer, lined
with aventurine ; has false bottom, and contains two
decorated smaller boxes. Lock and key. 6x9 inches.
1079 Same.
1080 Same.
1081 Same.
1082 Same.
1083 Same.

1084 GOLD and black lacquer tea-box, with lock and key ; two
square caddies, with sliding lids. 8x5 inches.
1085 Same.
1086 Same.
1087 Same.
1088 Same.
1089 Same.

1090 RED Sealing-wax lacquer box, ornamented with land-
subject in relief, silver-mounted, with lock and key,
containing six gold and black lacquer boxes. 12x14
inches.
1091 Another, exactly similar.
1092 Another ; similar, black sealing-wax ; same size.
1093 Another ; same as last.
1094 BLACK sealing-wax lacquer tobacco-box, lined with tin-
foil, with tray for cigars. 5x7 ins.
1095 Same.
1096 Same.
1097 Same.

ADDENDA.

BRIC-A-BRAC.

1 ANTIQUE padlock, iron shell, with copper joints, massive and quaint to a high degree; Sixteenth century; in perfect order.

2 PAINTED iron casket, original lock and key, on wrought legs, 3x3 inches. Perfect.

3 IVORY inlaid casket, Sixteenth century; Italian. 4x8 inches.

4 WOOD carvings, Dutch figures; Seventeenth century. 9 inches high.   3 pcs

5 BRASS tankard, with cover (tin lining) engraved with the name of JOHANNES HOPER, etc., 1711; ornaments of crown and vase; extremely fine, without dent or flaw. Height, 12 inches.

6 PAIR of solid bronze candlesticks, Louis Quatorze style and age; elaborate ornamentation in high-relief. Height, 9 inches.   2 p

7 CRUCIFIX used in the Greek Church, long Russian inscription, view of a town, and seven figures, besides the Crucifixion on one side, the other side elegantly chased; solid brass; Seventeenth century. 9x7 inches. A fine and rare article.

8 TRYPTIC, extremely fine.

9 DYPTIC, with raised figures on all sides; extremely fine; brass.

10 VIRGIN MARY, small figure, in costume. Height, 14 inches.

11 BRASS placques; religious subjects.   :   2 pcs

12 CRUCIFIX; wood, brass-mounted. Height, 10 inches. Very fine.

13 —— Old bone carving.

14 HOLY Mother and Child, moulded and painted in gold and blue. 12 inches.

15 OLD oak carved-panels, Sixteenth century. 14x16 inches.
3 pcs

16 FINE old tray, wood, marquetry work. 12x18 inches.

17 PLACQUES, with busts of George III., Frederick Duke of York, George IV., and the Princess Charlotte, in frame; as one lot.

18 MEERSCHAUM pipe, silver-mounted bowl, long and handsomely polished and ivory-mounted stem; well-colored and valuable.

19 SHELL mounted as a receiver on stem of brass, with porcelain flowers; unique and beautiful.

20 COSSACK whip, perhaps the only one in the country; a curiosity.

21 FRENCH fan, handsomely painted, and carved in mother-of-pearl, the maker's name and date on one of the leaves; very elaborate.

22 IVORY carving, nude boy with lyre; a seated figure, very beautifully executed.

23 —— Cane head.

24 SNUFF-BOX, enameled porcelain, silver-mounted, and painted in bright colors; oriental.

25 —— Tortoise-shell in the form of a trunk, the mountings (silver) made to correspond to the trimmings of that useful article; old and very pretty.

26 —— Enamel on copper, silver-mounted; fine and rare.

27 —— Old Dutch horn, brass-mounted, curiously etched and painted; two verses in Dutch.

28 SCENT-BOX most beautifully carved out of a cocoa-nut.

29 PICTURE frames, tortoise-shell veneering. 2 pcs

30 JEWEL-BOX in the shape of an egg, French porcelain in gold and colors, the mountings copper gilt.

31 JEWEL-BOX, copper-enameled, beautifully painted with decoration of flowers, on three feet.

32 Similar to last, the feet wanting.

5

33 Saltcellar, white porcelain, with a painted rose on its
  stem for the cover handle, the other decorations in
  raised design ; triangular shape ; handle wanting.

34 Painted Italian saltcellar, blue ground ; fine.

35 Silver watch made by DeBefee, who made the chimes for
  the cathedral at Liege, in 1650. This is a repeater,
  with bell attached to the inner case, which, like the
  outer, is perforated in quaint and artistic patterns ;
  silver dial, Roman and Arabic numerals, original hands.
  A rare article, worth $50.

36 Box of lachrymatories, antique glass, Roman, large and
  small ; really fine.   6 p

37 Candlestick ; the nozzle on the top of a wild-boar's head ;
  beautifully carved in serpentine ; handle broken and
  well-mended ; extremely fine.

38 Vase of the same material, one vessel within another,
  united by a screw on stand, all ten inches high ; extremely fine and valuable ; Seventeenth century.

38* Female head in alabaster, miniature size.

39 Placque ; head of Diogenes in yellow marble, on breccia
  ground ; old and fine.

39* Antique heads in white marble, found at Cicero's Villa
  Tusculum, and presented by the Prince of Syracuse to
  the late Gov. Lyon ; extremely fine.   2 p

  [Two heads out of the same lot were sold with the effects of the
  late Hon. Charles Sumner, and brought a high price.]

40 Head of Leo X. (the Magnificent) in wax, in colors and
  gold, inclosed within case ; miniature.

  [This is a piece of Seventeenth century work entirely perfect and
  beautiful. All will agree with me that nothing equally fine of the
  kind has been seen among us. This is from the celebrated collection of the Abbe d'Otreepe de Bouvette, Liege.]

41 Miniature bust of Shakespeare.

42 Colored etching, Eighteenth century ; extremely fine ;
  small oval, in frame and glass.

43 MINIATURE landscape in oil ; extremely fine. (*Multum in parvo.*)

44 Same, in oil, on wood.

45 Same, Beggar and Child, with dog ; equally fine.

46 Same, Smoker with a firkin of beer.

47 Same, St. John ; gold and colors. Very fine.

48 Same, Charles I. of England.

49 Same, head of a lady, in carved Italian frame ; fine.

50 Same, Monkey as cook, on wood.

51 Same ; pair of landscapes in oil ; views on the Rhine, one by moonlight ; *gems.* 2 p

52 Same ; pair of landscapes, with many figures equally fine. 2 p

53 LANDSCAPE on panel ; view on a river ; good.

54 SKETCH by Philip, R.A., on · canvas, mounted on panel, after Rubens.

55 HEAD of a gentleman in military dress, on copper ; old and fine.

56 HEAD of Velasquez, by Phillips, R.A. ˙

57 HEAD of a monk.

58 CAVALIER and companion ; a pair. 2 pcs

59 SKETCH, Woman on a donkey, led by her husband.

60 ITALIAN peasant woman spinning ; masterly sketch.

61 DUTCH Burgomaster ; a sketch.

62 SKETCH, Queen Esther ; fine sketch.

63 —— Crusader. Fine.

64 —— after Rembrandt. Fine.

65 MODERN landscape. Fine.

66 COLORED prints, in frame, small, old. 2 p

67 CALLOT's Cruelties of war, a series of 18 etchings ; original ; valuable.

68 REMBRANDT's etchings. 34 p

69 OIL painting by Weenix, Dead game ; original and fine.

> [This is a valuable picture, and this note is only to call attention to what might otherwise be passed over as an unimportant item in the catalogue.]

70 FEMALE bust, a fine old Italian painting.

71 FISH piece, by Alexander Adrianzen, 1650 ; fine.

72 ENGLISH landscape.

73 SEA piece.

74 STILL life, by T. H. Collier (American); a first-class sketch in oil.

75 LANDSCAPE, English.

76 FOWLS, a pair of oil paintings on panels, 6x9 inches, signed JACQUE. 2 p

77 SELECTED engravings, several proofs; fine. 10 p

78 Another lot, small. 10 p

79 Same; indifferent lot. 16 p

--- --- —

POTTERY AND PORCELAIN.

80 BOWL, porcelain, with decorations of flowers in colors.

81 Same, two sizes, one with bronze glaze. 2 p

82 Same, with chrysanthemum and violets; Saxon mark; very fine.

83 Same, with handles and cover; blue delft, quaint pattern.

84 Same, shallow; fine blue; oriental fabric. 2 p

85 Same, square-oblong, with handles, without cover; decoration, flowers green and red; Italian; old and imperfect, but very quaint.

86 INKSTAND; old Italian.

87 SAUCERS; old China, bright colors; with cover. 5 p

88 Same, with cups; old Saxon, decoration of flowers in bright colors; fine set. 6 p

89 CUPS; old Saxon, two blue, and one cream white (with its saucer), with raised decoration; all rare and fine. 3 p

90 ORIENTAL cups and saucers; 4 of each; 2 slightly imperfect. 4 p

91 TEA-POT; decoration in gold and colors; quaint; old French porcelain; handle mended, otherwise without a nick.

92 Same; Oriental porcelain; finer, but imperfect, bright colors.

93 Same; Oriental, blue, old pattern and fabric.

94 Same; old Saxon; perfect, fine and rare.

95 CREAM Jug; old Saxon; perfect and beautiful; rare.

96 CUPS, with handle and cover; old Saxon, of the best period, as shown by the style as well as mark (star above two swords crossed.)

97 Repetition of last.

98 SUGAR-BOWL; old Leeds; with twisted handles, flowers in colors on drab ground. Rare and fine.

99 COFFEE-POT; same fabric and style. Slightly cracked.

100 CUP and Saucer; hard paste porcelain, with the mark of the Frankenthal factory established in 1775; with Chrysanthemums and vines in purple and red, with gold edging. Extremely beautiful; valuable.

101 Same; another pattern from same factory.

102 Same; old English, Dawson & Co.; stamp, rose, sham-rock, and thistle. Fine blue decoration on *outside* cups and *inside* saucer. Very rare and valuable.

103 Repetition of last.

104 Same; Oriental blue, very light fabric.

105 STRASBURG tea service; old and quaint.   3 p

106 CUPS and saucers; *colored glass*, modern Venetian (last century.)   2 p

107 Same; old Berlin; blue and gold; rare and fine.

108 SALT-CELLARS; old Italian; one held by a lady.   2 p

109 VASE; blue delft; spreading top; a pair.   2 p

110 Same; same fabric, bottle shape, close top.   2 p

111 Same; with covers.   2 p

112 Same; flaring tops; mended.   2 p

113 Same; a set; one with cover, slightly imperfect.   2 p

114 FRUIT BASKET, with plate; blue and white; Derby (Eng-land) mark. Very fine.

115 Same; another pattern.

116 PLATE; blue and gold, Bristol (England) mark, fleur-de-lis pattern in scallops. Diameter, 14 inches.

117 Same; old blue delft; yellow rim. Diameter, 15 inches.

118 BOWL, or platter; "Polychrome," Flemish. Diameter, 10 inches.

119 SAUCER (Saxon) and plate (Delft).   2 p

120 TEA-CADDY; Saxon; bright colors, yellow and purple roses and red chrysanthemums. Cover mended. Fine.

121 PLATE, blue delft; very deep, inclining to bowl shape. Diameter, 14 inches.

122 MAJOLICA figures; rare. 3 p

123 —— Dish in the shape of a rooster; broken, and skilfully mended, gaudy colors; rare.

124 GRE DE FLANDERS; pottle-pot, 10 inches high; narrow top, swelling belly; blue and grey; 17th century; extremely fine and rare.

125 Same; equally old and well preserved. Fine.

126 Same; smaller size; equally fine. 7 inches high.

127 Same; the front covered with raised medallion figures. Extremely fine. 7 inches.

128 STONE Jug, or bottle; raised vine; very quaint.

129 BELLARMINE, or long beard jug; a rare and perfect example of the "Galonier," 18th Century manufacture. 16 inches high.

130 Same; equally fine. Height, 10 inches.

131 BEER-POT with block-tin cover and bottom, rim, drab ground, with decoration in colors. Very fine.

132 Same; stone-ware; cover wanting.

133 Same; blue and brown; without cover.

134 Same; grey stone-ware, covered with short and deep indentations made in the potting.

135 Same; blue delft, with block-tin cover. Fine specimen.

136 Same; old Italian, in perfect preservation, with quaint and vivid decorations. Rare.

[One of the gems of the collection.]

137 BUTTER-dish with block-tin lock-cover, old Italian, blue and brown. 1710 stamped on cover.

138 BERLIN Jug, blue and white. Height, 11 inches.

139 MILK-JUG, with cover, blue delft.

140 SALT and mustard dish, with cover; Italian.

141 DELFT Jar, wanting cover. One of the finest pieces of pottery in the collection, and, although imperfect, valuable. Mark unknown.

142 GRE DE FLANDERS, holy-water fountain; small and fine.

143 Vases ; a pair, with flat backs perforated near top to hang on wall ; a hard paste and fine glaze, with decorations of flowers in blue on white, called the " Royal blue," of Indian manufacture. Very old and fine.   2 p

144 Same ; round, with spreading tops, Oriental porcelain, blue and white. Extremely fine.   2 p

145 Same ; fine blue delft, large size, with close tops and bottle shape.   2 p

146 Same ; tall, octagon shape, with flaring tops.   12 inches high.   2 p

147 Same ; similar in shape to 145 ; blue delft, 6 inches.

148 Same ; blue delft, close tops.   3 p

149 Picture of the departure of Hager and Ishmael on 24 tiles, sold as one.

[Made and signed by *Aalmis*, Rotterdam.]

150 Tiles in various colors ; old Dutch.   25 p
151 Same ;   do   do   25 p
152 Same ;   do   do   25 p
153 Same ;   do   do   25 p
154 Same ;   do   do   100 p
155 Same ;   do   do   150 p

Various ; Mostly Oriental.

156 German music-box for 6 tunes, discourses when you turn the handle.

157 Collection of Turkish short swords (knives).   11 p

158 Japanese knife, in lacquer case.

159 Japanese screen, silk embroidery ; mounted.

160 Chinese pictures on glass, black-walnut frames.   4 p

161 One, with the coat-of-arms of England,   do

162 Japanese ladies' belt-buckles.   3 p

163 Same ; ivory, mounted in bronze.   2 p

164 Turkish ; enamel,   do   2 p

165 Chinese crystal crosses, mounted in silver.   2 p

166 India ivory inlay card-case ; card size.   2 p

167 CHINESE ear-rings crystal; not mounted.   9 pairs
168 —— Charms, cut crystal;   do   29 p
169 —— Same; plain,   do   do   29 p
170 —— Soap-stone fancy box, with cover.
171 —— Ivory carved ear-rings; not mounted.   4 pairs
172 PEARL breast-pins; not mounted.   2 p
173 IVORY   do   carved in flowers.   3 p
174 ——   do   do   fine; in silk boxes.   3 p
175 —— Carved in various shapes.   6 p
176 CHINESE horn, club and riding whip.   2 p
177 PARIS crystal sleeve-buttons (1 pair not mounted).   2 p
178 CHINESE crystal crosses.   2 p
179 —— Scarf-pin; ivory.
180 INDIAN card case; ivory
181 TURKISH jewelry boxes; fine.   2 p
182 Same; with covers.   2 p
183 Same; medium size.
184 Same; with stand.   2 p
185 TURKISH enameled cups.   9 p
186 —— Porcelain cups, fine; one broken.   5 p
187 JAPANESE (Kaga) cups, enameled.   4 p
188 TURKISH portmonnaies and cigarette-case.   3 p
189 —— Cigarette-case.
190 —— Sheath, with two knives.
191 —— Filigrane silver set of jewelry; pin and ear-rings; the set.
192 —— Another set.
193 Same; silver gilt (pin and ear-rings).   2 sets
194 Two Japanese coins.
195 OLD flint-lock musket taken from the Rebels at Fort Fisher.
196 PAIR gilt spurs taken from the heels of a Rebel soldier at Shiloah; fine.
197 OLD sabre.
198 Another.
199 REAL Sardonyx cross. 3½ ins. long.
200 AGATE cane-heads. 1 broken.   3 p
201 SHELL and gilt card-basket, oval.
202   do   do   do   do
203   do   do   do   do
204   do   do   do   do

205 10 assorted etagere ornaments, gilt, etc.
206 10   do   do   do   do
207 10   do   do   do   do
208 10   do   do   do   do
209 10   do   do   do   do
210 10   do   do   do   do
211 10   do   do   do   do
212 10   do   do   do   do
213 12 assorted size pocket compasses, gilt.
214 SHELL work-box. 9x6 ins.
215 Very rich and large specimen of Opal in matrix.
216   do   do   do   do   do
217   do   do   do   do   do
218 2 do   do   do   do   do
219 4 Fine large   do   do   do
220 5   do   do   do   do
221 5   do   do   do   do
222 17 OPALS, assorted, ready for mounting.
223 13   do   do   do
224 10   do   do   do
225 2 Boxes Oriental shells.
226 FINE painting on ivory ; Vestal Virgin.
227 FRUIT-LIFTER, gold-lined, sterling silver.
228 OLD blue delft plate with Dutch inscription.
229 JEWEL-BOX, pearl basket-work mounted in ormulu ; oval.
    5x6 ins. Fine.
230 BUCK-HORN and ivory stand, handsome carving. Height,
    8 ins.
231 ELK-HORN match-box, with bas-relief figures in white.
    Height, 4 ins.